I Am a Ghost Hunter

By Mike Roberts

Alameda Free Library
1550 Oak Street

FOREWORD

As there are many more folks interested in the field of research in the supernatural otherwise known today more so as The Paranormal, we often encounter the positive with the negative in such said upsurge. The curiosity of the unknown is nothing new and because of the rise in cable shows and books doesn't mean that is the sole reason as to why. One would have to be a fool to believe that and so I refer those serious about the field to this reading material, a book well worth its weight in knowledge. Nowadays, one can call themselves a paranormal investigator, create a group and get some equipment and off they go believing they are a real Ghost Hunter. The further can be from the truth as Author Michael J. Roberts demonstrates as to why in this book, "I Am A Ghost Hunter". The author combines his twenty-plus years of field research and committed on-going tasteful practices along with personal moments to attest to the real reality of searching for answers as human beings. If you're interested in learning the many ways and methods of researching the unknown from true accounts and personal testimonials without all the hogwash of reality television...then this is a read for you!

-Author, Alexandra Holzer

PROLOGUE

Ever since I was a kid I can remember being interested in the paranormal. Growing up, I experienced several incidents that led to a greater interest in the strange things happening everywhere. Where I am today is what has become of an early fascination gone rampant, becoming almost obsession. Years, money, and other aspects of my life became consumed within the search of looking for answers. I can remember the first incident like it was yesterday.

I grew up in the small town of Wilmington, North Carolina. Birthplace of Michael Jordan and home to Hollywood East. A small town on the southeast border of North Carolina. It is lined with beaches, a historic waterfront downtown area, and nests one of the most haunted locations in the world. The Battleship North Carolina.

Wilmington is rich in its history of slavery, civil war, and has a lot of the prime ingredients that most people will find when looking for haunted locations. I guess you could say it was an ideal place to grow up if you have a fascination in the paranormal, but truthfully, it was none of these things that got my interest.

Twenty four years ago, my family moved into a new house on the south side of town. For a while it was only my parents and I. I was eight years old, and in a new unfamiliar environment, having to make new friends, attend a new school, and find ways to keep myself busy.

Just after moving into the new house, my uncle went through a pretty rough divorce. He and his children, Richard who was my age, and Shannon who was a little younger than us, all moved into the house with us. I was excited to have my cousins living there. It made it more fun to be around the house when you have people your own age to play with.

Richard and I shared a room. Shannon, being a younger girl, shared the room in the back with her father. We were typical kids. Our room became the "clubhouse" and no girls were allowed. We even had a sign on the door to emphasize this rule. It wasn't that we disliked playing with Shannon, but boys will be boys.

One late afternoon, my parents were at their respective jobs, while us kids were under the care of my uncle. Richard and I were in our room playing board games and listening to music. After a while, we heard a knock on the door. My uncle came in and sat down. He explained to us that Shannon felt left out because we excluded her from everything, and that she was having just as hard of a time with the transition in lifestyles as we were. He asked us, nicely, to find something we could all play together.

After an hour or so of debating what we should do, Richard and I went into the living room. Shannon was sitting in her father's lap, wearing one of his old red and black flannel shirts, as he was reading a book to her.

Being the type of boys we are, we agreed to play a game with her. We told her we would play hide and seek, but she would have to be "it". Before she could argue, we ran into the back portion of the house.

The house was set up in a manner that one large room had been divided into two rooms. A small narrow hallway was built to divide the rooms. The back room had its own entrance way, and its own exit to the outside of the house. Both rooms had access to the closet space, which opened from both sides. We promptly hid in the closet, knowing that if she made the mistake of heading down the narrow hallway, she could not turn around quick enough to chase us and we could make a run for the living room.

After a short period of waiting and trying to be as quiet as possible, we heard the sounds of someone heading towards the back of the house. We peeked through the cracks in the closet door to see who it was, and in which direction they went. We saw the red and black flannel shirt pass the doorway and make the turn going to the narrow hallway. We both got excited that she had gone the wrong way, and prepared ourselves to run like bats out of hell once she got far enough into the back room. We heard the footsteps coming ever so slowly down that narrow hallway which was just to the left of the side of the closet I was standing in. We heard the back door open and now knew she was past the point of no return. We flung the closet doors open and almost ran each other over trying to hustle into the living room.

As we rounded the corner, we both stopped dead in our tracks. Our mouths dropped to the floor. I looked at Richard, and he had a very confused expression on his face. When I looked up, there was Shannon. She was still sitting on the couch in her dad's lap, reading the book together. She had decided she was not going to play because she didn't want to be "it".

As you can see, this was a shock to us because not only did we both see what we thought to be her, but we heard it. We heard the footsteps, we heard the door open. There was absolutely no way she could have turned around in that room, made her way down the narrow hallway, and get so far ahead of us that she could have gotten back into position on her dad's lap before we made it in there.

As I began explaining to my uncle what we had just seen, he tried to shut us down pretty quickly. He told us Shannon had been in there with him the whole time. He thought we were joking and trying to scare her into not wanting to play with us. We were dead serious. It definitely happened. After a few minutes of explaining the story several times, he began to show concern that someone might have broken into the house through the side door. He told us to stay put and he walked through the house to try and find evidence of an intruder.

He came back after only a couple of minutes and confirmed

that there was no one else in the house.

At that point, the three of us went outside and played in the backyard.

During the time that my cousins continued to live in the house, we always had a fear of that back room and would never go back there alone. Most of the time, we wouldn't go back there together either.

This was the first time I can ever remember this type of thing happening, but where it all led after that got more and more interesting.

THE BEGINNING

My childhood experience was just the first of the many things I would see during my lifetime that would baffle me. In elementary school, every so often, we would have book fairs. I was a huge fan of the movie GHOSTBUSTERS. At the book fairs they would always have the picture books based on the movie or even based on the Saturday morning cartoon. Every time one of these book fairs would come up, I had so much excitement built up in me that I could barely sit still at my desk.

In fourth grade I remember going into the book fair and looking for one of the GHOSTBUSTER books. This year, they didn't have any. What they did have, was books, with pictures in them, of "real" ghosts. They were pictures that were taken by people who had been in a haunted house, or who had taken a picture and noticed something strange that wasn't supposed to be in the photo.

I picked up one of these books and immediately bought it. I was fascinated. These pictures proved that ghosts were real. My young mind at the time saw these as absolute proof. There was no way these could be fake or they wouldn't be allowed to be published, right?

Whether the photos were real or not, they were enough to open my interest into what the possibilities could be. Are ghosts real? Are the ghost stories true? How could someone get photos of a ghost or be in a haunted place long enough to see it? This really brought up some new and terrifying ideas.

I used to walk home from school every day. It was only about 7 blocks, but it was an everyday ritual. About a block from my elementary school, I always had to turn left onto a particular road with the most notorious name. Elm Street. At this age, I was very aware of the horror films and knew that this street in the neighborhood had that same vibe to it.

About halfway down the street on the left hand side was the only abandoned house. The other houses were nice, with clean kept yards, fences, dogs, and your stereotypical green grass. Right smack in the middle was a blue, run down, house that just seemed to be out of place. It was creepy. All the kids from school talked about it being a haunted house. We all believed it to be haunted.

By fifth grade, some friends and I finally decided we were going to do what no other kids had dared. We were going to go inside this haunted house.

When the school bell rang that day, I met two other classmates in the school yard, and we made our way down to Elm Street. As we approached the house, you could see the broken windows, collapsed front porch, and massive spider webs. I remember the walk up to the house, through the brown grass, sent a chill down my spine and every hair on my neck stood on end.

At first, the three of us just stood on the front porch staring at each other, waiting to see who would be the brave one to go in first. After a few moments of deliberation, I took the first step through the broken front door. When I first entered, the interior was in shambles. There was what looked to be a really nice staircase that had broken and collapsed, so there was no access to the second floor. The floor was covered in thick grey dust. Bugs were crawling just about everywhere inside the house, and the carpet had moss growing in it. There was still furniture and some personal belongings like clothes and toys. It was as if someone had just picked up and left without taking anything with them.

I inched my way further into the house. In what used to be the living room, there was a small nightstand with a picture of a family. I didn't want to touch anything or disturb the layout of anyything in the house. I looked back and noticed my other two classmates had still not come in the house. The further in I went, they began to make their way in. I guess they were waiting for me to find out if it was safe. If no ghost had come and grabbed me yet, it must be safe.

As we all worked our way to the center of the house, we began to hear noises. Things that creaked. Things that banged. We got a little spooked, but knew that it was probably just the old house making noise. After all, it was in horrid condition. Even though it was only three o'clock in the afternoon, the inside of this house was almost completely dark. One of my classmates spotted a toy motorcycle on the ground near the fallen staircase. He walked over to pick it up. As he got close to the staircase we heard a loud moaning noise. It was terrifying. The other classmate dropped his book bag and ran out of the house. My curiosity wanted to know where the moan came from. Personally, I thought maybe someone was still living in the house and they knew we were trespassing, so they were trying to scare us off. Nonetheless, he reached down to pick up the motorcycle. After it was in his hands, he turned to me and breathed a sigh of relief.

Just as he began to start walking towards me, we heard a loud shrieking scream. It startled both of us. What followed next, sent us both flying out of the house in tears. A strong woman's voice screamed "JONATHAN!!!" Neither of us were named Jonathan, but we didn't stick around to find out whose name it was.

When we finally stopped running, we both sat down. Our other classmate was nowhere to be found. I saw that he was still holding the motorcycle. He tried to give it to me, but at first I wouldn't take it. I was too afraid that if I had the motorcycle, it would cause the "ghost" to follow me.

By the time we got ready to finish walking home, I took the motorcycle from him, and told him that when I walked to school the next morning I would put it back inside the house.

The next morning, on my way to school I walked past the Elm Street house and stopped in front. I attempted to walk into the yard and up to the porch again, but the fear from the incident wouldn't let me. My legs felt like they were frozen in place. I walked as far into the yard as I could and threw the motorcycle through one of the already broken windows. I heard it bounce off something and hit the floor.

During the school year, if you got caught with something at school you weren't supposed to have, teachers would confiscate it and keep it in their desk drawers. This particular year I was looking forward to getting my Teenage Mutant Ninja Turtle cards back, along with several other things I had gotten caught with. On the last day of school, the teacher pulled the box out from under her desk that was full of all the treasures taken from the kids throughout the year. Seeing everything in that box all together was like a kid's dream toy chest. Everything from walkmans to G.I. Joe figures.

After getting my stuff back and getting over the excitement of finally seeing my beloved items again, I looked around the room to see what some of the other kids had gotten back. I noticed one of the classmates that had gone into the house with me had an expression on his face I couldn't explain. He looked pale white, sweating, and as if he might vomit. The last bell rang and we all ejected into the halls of the school for the last time before we started middle school.

I walked up to my disturbed classmate to see if he was okay. He attempted to talk to me but was on the verge of tears. I thought maybe something he had taken from him earlier in the year had gotten broken in the pile, or he never got it back at all. When I asked him the third time, if he was okay, he reached in his pocket and pulled out what the teacher had handed back to him. It was the motorcycle from the house on Elm Street.

I have no idea how he came back into possession of that motorcycle. I know for one hundred percent certainty that I threw it into that house. I was the last one to school that day, and when I got there, he was already in his seat, so I know he didn't have time to go into the house before school and get it back. This wasn't a motorcycle that looked like the one in the house. It was the actual motorcycle. With the name Jonathan written on the side of it in crayon.

INSPIRATIONS

Throughout middle school, the paranormal expeditions took a spot on the back burner. I was becoming more interested in what other people had experienced, and to see if any of their stories were like mine.

One of the most popular unexplained occurrences where I grew up was the infamous Maco Light. Anytime you heard anyone talk about their experiences eight out of ten people talked about their experiences seeing the light. No one was ever quite sure of the light, what it was, where it came from, but there was no doubt that it was there.

The legend behind it is about a train conductor named Joe Baldwin. In the 1800's, Joe Baldwin was said to be the victim of a horrible train accident. Joe ran the caboose. The train was just short of the station in Maco when it ran into problems. They uncoupled the caboose and pulled the rest of the train up to the station for repairs. Joe was told to stand watch with a lantern so that as the train backed up to reconnect, they would have a reference point on the distance. As he waited for the other half of the train to return, another train was approaching fast from the other side. The oncoming train could not see the lonely caboose in the dark. Joe frantically swung his lantern back and forth to no avail as the oncoming train never saw him and smashed into the caboose. The legend says Joe Baldwin was thrown from the caboose and decapitated. People believe that the Maco Light is actually the ghost of Joe Baldwin swinging his lantern to try and find his missing head.

This light had become so famous that the government had actually shut down the area to try and explain the lights. No explanation was ever given. They were stumped. In 1965 famed parapsychologist and author, Hans Holzer, made a trip down to try and figure out the mystery. He never witnessed the light himself, but he took down and documented numerous eye witness reports of people who had seen the light first hand.

The light has been seen by literally hundreds of people,

including President Grover Cleveland. Once the tracks were dug up in 1977 the reports of the light pretty much vanished.

This particular story leads into two directions. Middle school, and about 5 years ago. I am only going to talk about one path in this chapter and cover the information about the Maco Light investigation in another chapter.

Eighth grade left me with a huge amount of questions when it came to ghosts. I found the Maco Light to be the most popular and common story from people in Wilmington and the surrounding areas. I did a quick search on ghost books in the local library, and that one event led to the greatest influence for me. Hans Holzer.

I picked up a copy of Holzer's book entitled "Ghosts I've Met". This was the first type of these kinds of books I had ever sat down and read. I immediately thumbed through the book to find the chapter on the Maco Light. I could not believe that an incident had drawn so much national attention, yet was still never explained. Dr. Holzer believed that Joe Baldwin did not realize he was dead, and was still warning the oncoming trains.

The more I read about his experiences, all documented, the more I wanted to be just like him. His investigation methods were cutting edge. He used a tape recorder to capture voice phenomenon, he used a trance medium to hold conversations with the other side, and he used very genius methods such as baby powder to detect objects moving on their own. He was a true pioneer. I continued to read and follow his work all the way through high school, but in ninth grade, it led me to my first investigation.

There have not been many people who have influenced me to do what I do more than the works of Dr. Holzer. Saturday nights were spent at my grandmother's house watching Unsolved Mysteries. The mixture of seeing so many unexplained things, and the determination of people like Hans Holzer, left me wanting more answers. Answers I could not find through the experiences of others. I began to realize that with so many strange things going on, the answers were never there.

Unsolved Mysteries was the biggest television influence. I remember countless nights of staying up to watch it, then being too scared to fall asleep, or even too scared to get up and walk to the bathroom in the dark. It was a feeling of fear, but with the fear came adrenaline. It was a rush. The same way that people fall in love with a roller coaster. The fear makes the ride fun. For me, this was my roller coaster.

The main thing I learned from Dr. Holzer was to document everything. Interview the client and listen to important details in their stories. It goes beyond that, however. Because of Dr. Holzer, I bought my first cassette tape recorder, and went in search of my own voices from the dead. I also used this to record people telling me their strange and interesting stories. I kept notebook upon notebook of all the information given to me by people who had been through what they considered a haunting.

This stuff was beyond the books I had been reading before. These were obviously on a more advanced level and not just your average ghost story book. This was the first time I had seen a book with a serious investigation method. This opened up an entirely new world for me. The possibilities were endless. It was the first time I had ever seen someone who did this as a professional and put so much work into their research. Was this going to be the breakthrough to finally help get the answers I have been starving for? It was definitely a start. This led to my first organized "team" for investigations. We now had some new knowledge and a great start on how to make the approach, and possibly find ways to improve the current methods or adapt them to our own. Ninth grade was an exciting time indeed. This is where my serious journey begins. I have spent the years since then traveling the country and chasing stories of haunted locations. I have been to places people consider to be the most haunted locations in the world. These are some of the stories from the locations that intrigued me.

Some of the things I have seen I cannot explain, but I always look for an explanation first. I pride myself on my abilities to look for everyday reasons to things that most consider to be paranormal. Do not confuse my beliefs of the paranormal with the approach I take. I am what they consider a skeptical believer. We do not have to convince a believer, but we do have to convince a skeptic. So while I may truly believe something to be paranormal, if I have doubts about what the skeptic would say, I have to throw it away. I have to think like a skeptic. What would a skeptic do on this investigation? If I show this to a skeptic, what will be the first question they ask, and did I check to make sure I know the answer to that question? I find that using this technique of investigating as a skeptic actually makes me a better investigator, and more credible in my research. If I know deep down in my heart that it was something paranormal, but not enough proof to convince a non believer, then I consider it my personal experience.

THE HOUSE IS STILL HAUNTED

When I was fifteen, my little brother was seven. We still lived in the same house I had that first experience, only now, the entire back room was mine. A few years had gone by, but I never forgot that original experience. Sometimes it would make it hard for me to sleep at night. There were so many unexplained noises in the house, and I constantly would hear footsteps coming down that narrow hallway to my room door. Sometimes my heart would beat so hard I could feel the bed shake.

My little brother stayed in the room on the other side of the closet. He was very afraid of the dark, but most of all, he just thought my room was cool. He always tried to spend as much time hanging out with me before bedtime as possible. We would play video games, watch movies, and stay up all night. It was paradise to a kid.

I remember coming home from school one day, being in the house alone before my parents got off work. I was sitting in the living room and I kept hearing what sounded like footsteps walking towards the living room from the back of the house. As I would look down the hallway to see if anyone was coming, the bathroom door opened on its own. Then I heard a loud bang the next room over. I was so frightened that I went outside of the house and actually sat on the sidewalk until my parents got home. I did not want to be in there alone.

Needless to say, there was definitely something going on in the house, and had been for years. The house has different vibes when you walk into it. Sometimes it can feel perfectly fine, and other times, it can feel like you shouldn't be there.

One night particularly, after hours upon hours of video games, it was getting late and I told my little brother he would have to go to his own room because I was tired and getting ready to go to sleep. As always, he put up a little bit of a fight, challenged me to one more game, and off to bed he went. After about an hour of lying there in the quiet, and dark, I heard him call my name. I answered him and he asked, "Did you hear that?" I told him that I did hear it. He was referring to what sounded like a scraping noise coming from within the closet that separated the two rooms. All of a sudden, something fell with a thud. I heard the footsteps barreling down the hallway. I opened my door and there was my brother. "Can I sleep with you tonight?" he asked. I knew he was scared and to be honest, I was a little freaked out as well.

He climbed up into my bed and we turned the television on to try and watch something to take our mind off the noises. Just when we were both about to fall asleep, we heard a different noise. He looked over and tapped me on the shoulder. When I looked, the closet door had come open by itself.

Living in North Carolina, especially on the coast, you get familiar with the hot summers and the humidity. This particular night, I had a box fan on the floor, turned on, to keep the room cool at night. The closet door had come open about eight inches. There was no way this could have been caused by the fan or the small vacuum of air generated by the fan. We again heard some scuffling inside the closet. My first thought was that it might be a mouse. It wouldn't be unheard of. Just as we started to settle down again, more shuffling and movement came from the closet. I turned the volume down on the television to try and hear it. The room was completely dark other than the light coming from the television.

I turned the television off and everything was eerily quiet. The only sound in the room at this point was the fan. All of a sudden, a very loud shuffling, like something moving with a purpose came out of nowhere. The box fan fell over and there appeared to be something standing or sitting on top of it. We were both looking at it, scared to death. You could definitely make out the shape of a head. It turned and looked at us with two glowing eyes. My brother was so scared he couldn't move. I told him I was going to count to three, then throw my pillow at it, and run for the light switch. He begged me not to make any sudden movements, or do anything that would make whatever it was attack us. He referred to it as a GREMLIN. It kind of looked like one in the darkness. I counted to three, slowly lifted the pillow from underneath my head, and with all my might, hurled the pillow at the thing sitting on top of the box fan. I leapt out of the bed and sprinted to get the light on.

Once the light was on, there was nothing to be found. The box fan was laying flat on the ground and spinning loudly. My brother was securely hidden under the covers until I told him it was safe. I looked all around the room, but could not find a trace of what it could have possibly been. It had two glowing eyes that looked right at us and even blinked a couple of times. I opened up the closet door a little more than it already was and looked inside. Stuff had fallen over, and things had absolutely been moved around as if something had come through the closet. How we got to sleep after that is still a mystery to me.

After that night, my brother and I slept with the lights on most of the time. When the lights were on, the noises were gone. We never saw anything like that again the entire time in that house. So many strange things happened there.

Even in my later years, I have never investigated the house. I have kind of made it an unspoken rule to never investigate the places I live in. Not sure why I put that in place, but sometimes I just feel better off not knowing. My parents still live in that house, and as recently as me starting this book, they are still experiencing things there. Earlier this year, I watched the house while they went to Vegas for my dad's birthday. Things began to pick up when I was alone in the house. I saw an object move on its own. A power drill that was lying in the floor, ended up on a tabletop, and turned directions in the middle of the night. I saw it when it moved. While sitting in the living room, the bathroom door opened on its own.

When my parents got back in town, I told them about some of the things that happened while they were gone, and they didn't act surprised at all. A few days later, my dad was in the living room alone and saw the bathroom door not only open, but close, all on its own. He checked for drafts and other possible reasons on why it could have happened, but he couldn't figure it out. My dad has always been a bit of a skeptic. He doesn't believe in ghosts at all, but he has seen strange things, and he is one of the eye witnesses to the Maco Light. The one thing he will admit to being his only supernatural experience.

THE BIRTH OF RESEARCH: PARANORMAL

At fifteen you are very limited to the resources you can obtain in the hobby of the paranormal field. Together with my good friend Jason, we decided it was time to go out and start trying to find ghosts. So many people had experienced them, and there were so many stories and photos, we felt they had to exist. This couldn't just be mass hysteria. Jason and I decided we would find out for ourselves.

Jason didn't live far from me. He lived in a small apartment complex on the other side of the lake down the street from me, but there was a shortcut to getting to and from his apartment. Just behind his apartments was a cemetery. I have several family members buried in that cemetery and the family plots are there for the future. We took the tape recorder and a 35mm camera and ventured out into the cemetery just around dusk one evening after school. We only owned one other piece of equipment at the time, an electromagnetic field detector. The theory involving electromagnetic fields is that when a ghost tries to manifest itself, it will manipulate the EM field, causing the needle on the meter to fluctuate.

We set out on our course and found a good spot to start an EVP session. We spent a total of about two hours wandering from place to place letting the meter guide us. After being there for a while, we decided to call it a day and head back to his apartment and listen to the audio we had just recorded. Being outdoors and at a cemetery next to a busy highway, most of the audio was distorted or unusable. Things that sounded like they could be faint whispers were quickly dismissed. It's very hard to control the environment outdoors, much less, in a public location with a minimum amount of equipment and resources. We spent a couple of hours listening to the audio, rewinding and fast forwarding, before we hit our first catch. Jason had asked a question and there appeared to be an answer on the audio recorder. "Do you miss your family?" Jason asked. The reply was quick, and in direct response. A male voice, not our own, replied "I love them". We were literally excited and scared at the same time. It was a feeling of mixed emotions bound with sadness that someone might actually be missing and loving their family from beyond. There wasn't much more on the tape that could be deciphered but we were definitely pumped up to have caught this one that was undeniably loud.

Over the course of the next year, before Jason moved away, we continued to visit abandoned locations, graveyards, and experiment with the Ouija Board. Today as an investigator, I do not use Ouija boards, and it has nothing to do with them being dangerous, but because of the possible human contamination during the research. I will touch more on that subject later.

By the time I was seventeen, we had accumulated a couple of new recruits who shared our same interest in the paranormal. Jason was hard to find a replacement for. We worked extremely well together, and I knew I could trust him to not fake things. Throughout the years Research: Paranormal became well established and has seen and trained over twenty different members. The current team has been together for five years, and the methods of investigation have been custom fitted for a well-oiled machine. Ironically, the new lead investigator who heads up the team with me, is also named Jason.

Our team is broken down into several different parts. We didn't want to be so scientifically minded that we closed out the mystery of the metaphysical. After all, it was the stuff that couldn't be explained that got all of our interest in the first place. Using methods that have been tried and tested through the works of Dr. Hans Holzer, we integrated the old metaphysical investigative techniques with a scientific approach that has provided us with some very interesting results.

Jason, my lead investigator, has a background in film production and is a musician by trade. It helps to have someone who is familiar with cameras and their operations when trying to determine if an anomaly is caused by something completely natural with the camera. He also has a knowledge of audio production which helps when going through the hours of audio recordings.

Chad is our go to guy. He is well rounded in the metaphysical and with the technical side of things. He is very enthusiastic and the guy who is always willing to be used as a lab rat. He is a pharmacy technician which helps when dealing with clients. Sometimes medications can cause people to experience symptoms that they may interpret as paranormal. He is also a certified EMT, which helps in the case of any injuries or accidents while out in the field.

Key is our case manager. Her organization skills and ability to lead are unmatched. She is very technical, and can be very serious during investigations. She has a military background which allows her to take charge in any situation.

Lindsay is our metaphysical investigator. She goes into an investigation based on feelings and does not rely so much on equipment. The equipment she uses are technologies based on metaphysical studies and ITC communication. The ghost box, which is a device developed to do a linear sweep on a am/fm radio, is one of these tools.

At times we will use a team medium. Just as Dr. Hans Holzer used Ethel Meyers, we like to send our medium in to get an impression or reading of the location and make all of his/her notes prior to us entering the location. At the end of the night, after we have collected our data, we compare it to the impressions they have picked up on. At time, our medium is incredibly accurate, and while we do not rely on his/her abilities solely, it is a great addition. Our medium is well versed in the equipment and looks for correlating evidence to back up his/her readings. Our medium is also very science minded and will use all of the equipment to combine his/her efforts on an investigation.

Shellie was a trainee that was promoted to a full time member. Shellie really works well on both sides of the spectrum. She has been out on investigations with the team, and was trained from the ground up to be a part of the team. She had no prior training before hand, so she was custom made for the team.

Will is our team documentarian. He has a background as a filmmaker. He has most of his beliefs based in religion. He will follow the team around to document the case from start to finish on video. He is also an investigator who has been with me in some very tense situations.

The combination of people for this team make up an ingredient that helps us make a unique approach to the paranormal. It started with two kids who had a passion for the unexplained, and now has become a solid team that has opened up branches of the Research: Paranormal family all across the country.

PASS ME THE OUIJA, WOULD YA?

The Ouija Board is a heavily debated subject. Some people are afraid to use them for fear of bad and evil might overtake them. Others refuse to use them because there is too much human contamination involved, so you can never really know what to trust when you get "results" from it. The principle is simple. Two or more people place their finger tips on the edge of the planchette (a small pointing device), and it will spell out words using letters on the wooden board. A truly mystifying oracle. No one has been able to prove that ghosts manipulate this board in any form or fashion. Most likely the planchette moves without the users knowing due to small vibrations in the muscular system that will glide the planchette ever so lightly across the board.

I have had two experiences that involved the Ouija Board.

Nothing spectacular happened, but there were a few interesting details during the events that made it seem kind of odd. In my opinion, some modern day equipment is the same, or similar, as the Ouija Board. A few years ago a device referred to as the K2 meter was introduced to paranormal investigators. This device was a simple EMF detector that would light up in response to questions you would ask. I have heard people say they would never use an Ouija Board, but will see them parading around their K2 meter. Both items are used for the same purpose. Communication with the unknown through a physical medium. Whether it be the board, a K2, or even a voice recorder, the premise is the same. Asking something to communicate with you, using something other than a direct communication. Some people will say it's the intent of a user when it comes to the Ouija Board, and if that is true, then wouldn't it mean no matter what the communication medium is, the intent would still be there same? So no matter what was used, the intent is what would be dangerous, and not the medium itself.

At any rate, the first experience I had involving an Ouija Board, did not kill me, harm me, or follow me home. The last year of middle school, eighth grade, made way to a new student. Amanda had moved to Wilmington from Kentucky and came in after the school year had already started. I remember I had an instant connection with her. She was pretty, friendly, and very smart. We quickly became friends, and I can honestly say I may not have passed math that year had it not been for her.

One day in class she passed me a note. I excitedly opened it up and read that it was an invitation to her birthday party. I was honored to be invited. I knew a few of my other friends were going to be there as well, and Amanda was just an extremely fun person to be around.

I arrived at the party, late as usual, and was shown the way to the back yard. I remember hearing ROB ZOMBIE music playing from a boom box. As I rounded the house, I saw she had a huge trampoline with a rope hanging from a tree. Everyone was jumping on it, grabbing the rope, and swinging across the yard. It was a beautiful day outside. After a while of hanging around and being kids, we all went inside to give out the presents and have the typical traditions of cake eating and singing songs.

As typical kids would do, most of the guys hung out together, and most of the girls formed their own group. Amanda went to her room and came back with a small box. She laid it out on the table and I could hear the deep sighs from a few of the party attendees. There on the table was the first Ouija Board I had ever seen in person. I had seen all of the commercials that had come on the television with the kids playing, asking questions, and accusing each other of moving it. Amanda took the board out and set it up. A few of them gathered around, putting their hands on it. It was eerily silent. No one spoke. Some of them acted as if they were too scared to even breathe. After a few minutes of asking questions, it happened. The planchette began to slowly move. During this, each person with their finger lightly on the edge began to accuse the other of moving it. It began to move faster. Amanda spoke frequently about a "ghost girl" who lived in the attic named Ursula.

Amanda asked who was making it move. It slowly moved to the letter "U", then slid to "R", and by the time it go to the "S", Amanda and the rest let go. I could tell she was upset and scared at the same time. She told us the whole story about how she was often visited by Ursula and that at times, Ursula could be very mean. She quickly put the board away, and asked what else we would like to do.

The little bit of response had our adrenaline pumping for the supernatural, so we all decided to try the "Bloody Mary" trick. The legend behind this was that you going into a dark room with a mirror, stand in front of it, say the name "Bloody Mary" three times, and then when you turn on the light, the ghost of Mary, all bloodied, would be standing behind you. All of the girls decided to go first. They went into the bathroom as a group and turned off the light. The guys thought it would be funny to hold the door shut so that they wouldn't be able to get out. It would create a little bit of a fun panic. As we stood outside the door and heard them saying the chant, we stood ready. Just as they said it on the third time, the loudest crack of thunder I have ever heard in my life echoed through the house. The power went out and we all let go of the door. The sounds of the girls screaming could be heard from a mile away. We heard them grab the doorknob, try to turn, but it was jammed. The door would not open. Amanda's parents grabbed a screwdriver to try and pry the door open, and just as they got to the door, the power came back on and the door flew open. The girls trampled each other trying to get out of the bathroom.

It had been a beautiful day outside, but now there was one of the worst storms I had ever seen sweeping through the area. The original plan was that Amanda's party was supposed to be a sleep over. The weather was now so bad, that all of our parents were called to come pick us up. Most of us were picked up late because our parents didn't want to drive in such bad weather conditions. As I rode home, I thought about how spooky the experience was. It was probably all just coincidental, but the timing was perfect. After all, it is North Carolina. The motto here is "If you don't like the weather, just wait 5 minutes." But what about the door? Why didn't it open? Maybe because we had pulled it so hard that it jammed shut. Maybe the girls in a panic accidentally locked themselves in. Sounds logical. I still don't understand how the door only came open after the lights came back on. It was definitely a mystery to me, and an experience I will never forget.

Only one other time, did I have anything strange with this board. My parents had gotten me one for Christmas one year. They saw the commercials and knew I would want one. Now I had one of my very own. I never understood how Parker Brothers was able to license such an evil and dangerous object. Can you feel the sarcasm?

My ninth grade investigating buddy, Jason, came over one afternoon and we decided to give the board a shot. We used to have one of those huge aluminum garages behind my house. It was like something out of a horror movie. It stood over eighteen feet tall, and had two barn style doors on the front. The inside of it was huge. It was about the size of a small one bedroom house. The garage was very old and in poor condition. It was covered with large rust stains, the floor was half dirt and half concrete. We mostly used it for storing old junk and Christmas stuff, but it made for an awesome clubhouse. It had electricity, but it was minimal.

I had an old child's size pool table in there. It was small and made out of plastic, but it had felt on the table just like a real one. Jason and I decided this would be a prime location for us to set up our Ouija Board session. I had a few tea light candles, so we headed into the garage, placed the board on the table, and lit the candles. It was almost dark outside, so it made for a great atmosphere. We sat there for nearly two hours with no results.

Jason decided he was going to play a trick on me. He looked up and made a face of concern as if something was behind me. I turned quickly and looked. He laughed. What was behind me was a beam of light, which looked like it was coming from outside of the garage. Because the floor was mostly dirt, you could see the dirt particles churning inside the beam of light like a whirlwind. At first glance, it was a little spooky, but I understood that Jason was just teasing me. It had been almost three hours, so we blew the candles out and headed outside.

Jason went home and I went inside. After about an hour, something struck me as odd. It was dark out the entire time we were in the garage. Where did that beam of light come from? There were no street lights, and the moon wasn't bright enough to shine a beam that intense through a hole in the garage. The next morning I began to look around the building to see where the light might have come in from. Even with the garage being as old as it was, one thing it did not have, was holes. I immediately called Jason and asked him to come over. He also looked around and for the life of us we could not figure where the light had come from. We waited until it was dark out again and decided to run an experiment. I went inside the garage as Jason stood outside with a deer hunting light, which is a high powered flashlight. He tried shining it all around but to no avail. I never saw a shred of light. We switched places. I pointed the light into every crack I could find. Still nothing. It left us both scratching our heads.

I can't sit here and tell you it was a ghost. I have no idea what it was. The best I can explain it, it looked like the light you see in the movies when someone is going to Heaven. That light that shines down and pulls people up away from their bodies. Jason had seen that light, and without thinking it could be anything strange, tried to use it as a prank. Now it felt like the prank was on us. These couple of stories are the only things I have ever really had happen to me while in the presence of an Ouija Board. It didn't spin in a figure eight. No bubble came up in the viewer. As you can see, I did not die.

I truly believe the Ouija Board is the subject of a lot of hype, but mostly superstition. Sometimes people are too afraid of things, simply based on stories they have heard from others, and it discourages them from trying it and experiencing it themselves. I have never seen a published article or death certificate that read "Death due to Ouija Board Use/Exposure" and I am sure that they would be yanked off the toy store shelves if there were any proof that they actually worked the way people think they do. I guess I will never understand that hundreds of people are out to prove the existence of something beyond our world and understanding, but do not want to use the device they claim is the one item that opens portals and gateways. Seems like that would be the easiest way to prove there is another side. Put the board on a table, turn a camera on, and capture the proof. Sounds like, not only a very easy way to prove the paranormal, but to also prove that the board does in fact do the things that it's notoriously blamed for.

THE MEAT PACKING PLANT

I was sitting at my day job one afternoon when I got an urgent call. The mayor of Navassa, North Carolina was contacting us in regards to an old meat packing plant located just outside of Leland. Stories have run rampant there about ghost sightings and the location has been talked about for years as being haunted.

The plant was in operation from 1919-1923 and shut down shortly after the owner died. Legend says he was found in the center of the plant where he had hung himself. Through very thorough research, we found this not to be true. The owner had actually died of asphyxiation due to a gas leak in his home. Nonetheless, it became a popular location for teens to hang out in early seventies and eighties. Teens would sneak back onto the property, hidden deep in the woods off of a long stretch of dirt road, and party until dawn.

In 1982 a group of teens, who had spent the majority of the day hanging around the abandoned building, were witness to a grim tragedy. David Brown, of Wilmington, North Carolina, fell four stories to his death. The group of boys were trying to frighten each other. David was led to the top of the stairs where he lost his footing and fell straight down to the basement. There have been many other accidents in this location. The building is in such disrepair that the community of Navassa has been planning to tear it down and turn the property into a park.

After gathering some basic information about the location, we were promptly contacted by the State Port Pilot, a local newspaper for Brunswick County. They were to tag along to our investigation and report our findings into a special Halloween Edition of their newspaper.

To say this location would be a challenge is an understatement. With full permission from the mayor, we met the deputy sheriff who would turn the keys over to us and escort us to the gate that led down the long winding road to the plant. Upon arriving at the gate, the sheriff stated he would go no further. He warned us of large snakes, alligators, bears, and other predators that may be in the area. As we stepped out of the vehicles before proceeding, we were instantly met by hummingbird sized mosquitoes. Nature was not on our side. The only thing nature would provide for us that night would be the eerie glow of the full moon.

As we made our way through the woods and off the beaten path, the first glimpse of the meat packing plant came into view. It was massive. A huge four story building, missing walls, and barely recognizable, stood before us. The building had not had power for the last seventy years, so we relied on battery power for all of the equipment, and large torches and lanterns. The building still sat solid on the foundation. The only way up onto the foundation was a rickety old aluminum ladder that had been left behind. My team and I slowly made our way up and onto the main floor.

Looking around, it was easy to see how someone could get seriously injured. Being this far back in the woods, there was little to no ambient light. Seeing in the dark was almost impossible. At times, it would be so pitch black that even our high powered flashlights could not cut through the darkness for more than five feet. Each floor had a massive hole in it from where they could drop the animal remains straight down to the basement. There were several old elevators shafts, and dozens of narrow old stone staircases with no railing. It was visually stunning, yet scary. The wrong step on any floor would send you plummeting down into the concrete floor of the basement.

Each floor had a menacing look. Covered in graffiti, from people who had snuck into the building throughout the years, the walls seemed to tell a ton of stories. In the basement, something was really disturbing. There was an old concrete slab that was rumored to have been used as a satanic altar. It was covered in symbols and blood, and even had some hint of small animal remains littered around it.

We grouped together on the first floor and split into two teams. This location was large and dangerous so we wanted to make sure everyone was prepared. My team went straight down into the basement, and the second team went up to the fourth floor. As we began investigating, we immediately heard noises coming from the remains of an old elevator shaft. I walked over and sat an audio recorder at the bottom of the shaft and left it there to record for the rest of the night. I was accompanied by another investigator and one of the two news reporters. We split up on the basement floor and began to take photos. I was using a digital still infrared camera, and I noticed something in the far corner of the basement. I immediately called my other investigator over with his high definition night vision camera. I told him that I saw something move. My mind began to race. I wasn't even thinking about ghosts. I was thinking about what the sheriff had told us about bears. What I saw was a figure about six feet tall. As my investigator pointed his camera down and started shooting, there in the back of the room, appeared to be a torso and a head moving from right to left. It lasted about three seconds then disappeared. We were both shocked. There was only one way in the basement and one way out. We charged down to the other end. Nothing was there to be found. No person. No animal. Just empty room.

We made many attempts to try and figure it out. We suggested it may be a flashlight coming from one of our other investigators on a higher floor, but that would be impossible. What we saw with our eyes was black. We thought maybe it could have been an infrared illuminator shining down since it was picked up on the camera, but again would not explain why we saw it with our eyes, considering infrared is invisible to the human eye. Things had just started heating up, and we were only an hour into the investigation.

After a few hours, most of the initial activity started to die down. The investigators in the second group didn't have much luck with anything. We all regrouped on the first floor and decided to head back down to the basement. This time everyone came with us. It had started getting really late, and we were all beginning to get tired. The energy level of the team had reached a low point. Then out of the dark silent night, an investigator shouted to get our attention. We all hustled to the spot. It was the altar. Keeping in mind that this place has not had power in many years, and it far from civilization, we were confused at what was going on. The electromagnetic field detectors were lighting up in rapid succession when placed near or on the altar. The meters would buzz and alarm with intensity, then die off completely. One of the investigators began provoking. Provoking is used by some people to try and get a response through insult, or through saying things that would be relevant to the surroundings or time period of the assumed spirits. After each insult laid out by the investigator, the meters would respond louder and stronger. This continued on for about an hour. Shortly after, the activity had completely died off, so we called it a night.

It took a few days to get through a review of all of the

footage and audio we had recorded. There were voices on the audio that shouldn't have been there. There was the video captured of the figure walking across the back wall of the basement. There was the undeniable disturbance in the magnetic field. With everything we had been able to collect, we made the phone call to the news reporters that had been with us that night, and we gave them the story.

To my knowledge at the time I am writing this, the meat packing plant still stands. The mayor would like to restore the property as Navassa's first historic building. The friends and families of those who met a tragic fate there, would like to see the building torn down so that it would pose no threat, or invite harm to more people. This is a big concern with me. There were no trespassing signs posted throughout the property. The gate to get onto the road is locked and the key held by the sheriff. Can the building really be blamed for any accidents? This is why we stress that it is so important for people to get permission before attempting to investigate an abandoned property.

No credible ghost hunter or paranormal investigator would trespass or enter a location without proper permission. There have been other instances in the past where investigators have entered onto a property without permission and it has resulted in death. A few years ago, a group of two female would-be paranormal investigators parked their car in front of a house rumored to be haunted. They thought the house was abandoned. As they tried to enter the property, the owner came out with a gun and fired a shot, killing one of the girls instantly. Please take this warning to heart. If you want to be successful in this field, there are rules and ethics. Some of them could save your life.

THE BATTLESHIP NORTH CAROLINA

In October of 1961, the Battleship North Carolina made its way into Wilmington. After being decommissioned in 1947 it sat for fourteen years in New Jersey. In 1958 it was decided that the ship would be scrapped. Knowing that this was in no way fair to a ship that participated in every naval offense and earned fifteen battle stars, a statewide effort in North Carolina was made to give the ship a new home.

There have been many stories about ghosts on the battleship. Danny Bradshaw, the night watchman, has witnessed many things during his tenure. Enough that it prompted him to write his own book. I have spoken with Danny many times, and his stories are bizarre enough to make the hair on your neck stand up. His largest encounter was late one night while walking through the ship to turn the main power off.

He entered into the room where the main breaker is and reached to turn it off. He felt a hand on his shoulder. Thinking it was a buddy of his, he turned around. What he saw next would change his life forever. There, standing in the doorway, was a full bodied apparition. It was a man. Danny could see right through him. His head appeared to be made of flames. Danny screamed. He says the figure gave him a look that let him know, not to do that again.

Danny has had many encounters on the ship. The stories made it out into the public and skeptics have had a lot to say about his experiences. These stories have prompted paranormal teams from all over the world to travel to the ship to see for themselves.

A few years back, my team and I decided to set up an investigation and check out some of the claims ourselves. Driving up the ship, it is overwhelming. The ship is huge. It is visually stunning, and some areas can be the darkest spots you have ever been into. Many of the spots off the tour route have been off limits and untouched for years. It is a visually stunning place for a paranormal investigator, but can also be very dangerous. A wrong step can lead to falling down open ladder passageways in the floor, where you would land on one of the many decks below. It is full of overhead hazards, and things to trip over. If you are not careful, it could end your night early.

We have investigated the ship many times over the years, but one of the first times we ever set foot on it, work was being done on some of the lower decks, so there were areas we could not access. We set up our base location in the main hall and ran equipment into adjacent rooms. We focused our investigation on the infirmary, bullpen, mess hall, and chapel.

It's an old ship. It sits nested in the Cape Fear River in downtown Wilmington. It is immersed in water and spends all day baking in the hot sun causing the ship to act as a virtual oven. At night time, the ship cools down so many noises are expected in the process of the steel contracting. We heard many noises throughout the night but most could be explained away due to the nature of the location. Walking through the hallways and various corridors of the ship you can hear voices and whispers that seem to come from nowhere.

As usual, the team split into two groups. My group headed to the mess hall, and the others headed into the bullpen. It was relatively quiet. I entered the area where Danny Bradshaw had seen the man with the flaming head. This area is where the main power breaker is for the ship, so as to be expected, it was burying the EMF meters. Some people say that high levels of EMF can cause hallucinations, skin rashes, and other things to people who are sensitive to EMF exposure, however there are no studies to prove that this is true. Although an invention called the GOD HELMET, which bombards the brain with high intensity electromagnetic fields in a small confined area, did cause hallucinations to the wearer. This was the only study that seemed to prove the effect of EMF, but it would have to be an extremely large source, and concentrated directly into isolated parts of the brain. If it is in fact true that people who are hypersensitive to EMF experience the same effects, then it could possibly explain why Danny saw the man with the flaming head in this area.

We rotated the groups throughout the night in the different areas of the ship, but did not get much activity, until my group entered the bullpen. This was a relatively small room, with old rotary style phones piled on a small table in the center of the room. It appeared that the room was being used for storage as they worked on some of the other rooms down the corridor. For about an hour, my team and I sat in the dark with video and audio simultaneously recording. As we began to pack up to move to the next area, I asked for anyone to give us a sign if they did not want us to leave. Almost instantly, we heard the ringing of a phone. There were no phones connected, and the only phones in the room were in the pile on the table in front of us. It had an old time sound to it, almost the same as a kid ringing a bell on a bike. We all got really still and excited at the same time. I asked again for a sign. In the pitch black room, the phone sound echoed through the darkness. Two direct responses to the question asked. Did this mean something was in the room with us? After another half hour or so, we decided to leave the room since nothing else happened.

As we exited the bullpen, we met up with the other half of the group in the central meeting room. As we approached them, we were greeting by loud and excited investigators. They were huddled around one of the hand held miniDV cameras and grinning from ear to ear. One of the investigators brought the camera over. They had been in the mess hall and what they would show me next would be a perplexing find. As the investigator operating the camera was panning around filming the kitchen, a shadow in the shape of a person walked directly in front of the camera. It was fast, but you could definitely see the legs as it moved across the room. I could hear the investigator yell for the person to identify themselves but no one was there. We watched the footage several times, then headed back to the mess hall to try to recreate it. We used several forms of lighting including infrared and flashlights. We made over twenty attempts to recreate the anomaly with no success. It was very exciting indeed.

For most of the night we never even set foot into the infirmary. We had DVR cameras and audio recorders going the entire night, so we saw no real reason to put an investigator into the area while it was being monitored. Then team headed up to the bridge steering room and held an EVP session for about an hour, then regrouped and began packing up. It had been a long night, and we were looking forward to analyzing the footage.

During the data review process, we saw that we had collected some pretty unique things and made note of it all. I went through over 300 infrared digital still photos, and found one that was truly amazing. On the deck of the ship, I had fired off about 30 photos. In one of the photos appeared a phantom hand, it looked as if it was pointing to the entrance way to the mess hall. There was no way this could be an investigator hand as I was on the deck alone. It appeared to have a long sleeve as if it were coming out of a cloaked robe. The video of the figure walking in the kitchen was still looking like it would become our best piece of evidence. Still to this day when I watch that footage, I cannot come up with any rational explanation. We had ruled out lighting sources, shadows of other investigators, and plain old optical illusions. This piece was just going to have to stay unexplained. The most surprising of all the evidence was a three second audio clip caught on a digital recorder in the infirmary. We had made it a point to not go down there so we would have a completely controlled environment. For the most part it was completely quiet. The audio didn't even pick up a single creaking sound. About three hours into the recording I found the only sound the recorder picked up, the name PATTERSON, was said twice in a row, in a soft faint voice.

After going through everything, I phoned Danielle Wallace. Danielle is the programs director on the Battleship North Carolina. She is very knowledgeable about the ship and has access to all the records. I told her of the findings and sent her the audio clip. She did a cross check of the ship logs and found that over the course of time ten men with the last name Patterson had been assigned to that ship. That was all the information we could find and there was really no way to narrow it down to which of the ten men it could have been. At least that's what we thought. As I mentioned before, there were areas of the ship that were having work done, and were not accessible to us at the time. We returned to the ship a couple of years later and as Danielle walked us down to the brig, the ship's jail, I was shocked to what I saw next. On the inside of one of the cell walls, written in blood and feces, was "Patterson was here". The connection immediately clicked with Danielle, and she remembered the audio clip we had sent to her prior. This could be the Patterson we were looking for.

The team and I have investigated the battleship many times over the course of the last few years, and I must say it has never disappointed. Some of the hot spot areas on this ship are off the tour route, such as the bathroom and shower areas where the ship was struck by a Japanese torpedo and a couple of men lost their lives. There are many stories about the deaths of some of the men on that ship, but whether or not they are all lingering behind is yet to be determined. There is definitely something there. You can feel it from the minute you walk in. Keep your eyes open, your audio recording, and your video rolling.

CAUTION: CHILDREN AT PLAY

One of the most intriguing cases I have been a part of was just a few years ago. A friend of mine, Gabreael from Eastern Paranormal, referred a case to me about a friend of hers in Leland who was experiencing activity in her home that involved her fourteen year old daughter Jessica.

I made the initial phone call and interviewed the client, Phyllis, over the phone. They had all types of activity from full bodied apparitions to disembodied voices. The case particularly interested me because most of the activity was experienced by her daughter. Jessica talked about holding conversations with the entities in the house, as well as being physically touched. We agreed to make the case a priority and we assembled the team to head out.

After getting settled up, we did a walk-though and had Phyllis show us where the activity had taken place. This led us to multiple bedrooms, the living room, and a finished room above the garage. We asked that Jessica not be present for the first few hours, then we would bring her back in later. This would help determine if activity only happened once we brought her back into the house. I had brought out a smaller team this time to help control the situation. We wanted to be as thorough as possible.

We set up static video cameras around the house and began to split up into groups. One team would be upstairs, while the other team would be downstairs. In the room over the garage we placed a camera on a tripod against the far back wall, and an audio recorder on the dresser next to the camera. There was less than four feet between the two pieces of equipment. We placed another static camera at the bottom of the staircase, and one in the living room. We covered the entire house in audio recorders and began the investigation.

I was downstairs with one other investigator and we sat silently while the other two investigators upstairs held their EVP session. Within a matter of minutes we saw what appeared to be a shadow dart in front of the television and through a wall. I jumped up to inspect it, but could not find anything. There were subtle noises coming from the room we were in that sounded like footsteps walking across the floor directly in front of us. The night had started early, and the place was beginning to come alive.

From downstairs I could hear the booming voice of one of the investigators upstairs. He continued his EVP session for about an hour and then everything got silent. Just about the time I decided to call out to them to make sure they were okay, they began heading down the stairs. As I walked over, I could tell one of the investigators was shaken pretty badly. He looked as if he had run a marathon, then skipped about five months of sleep. He stopped halfway down the stairs and began to lean on the rail. He felt sick. A sudden headache had overcome him and he felt nauseous. We gave him permission to go home and as he packed his equipment up to leave, I had the other investigator that was with him take me to the spot where they were when he got sick.

We headed straight for Jessica's room. As we entered, there was an overwhelming smell of incense. Jessica had been burning incense in her room earlier and the smell was just over powering. I offered this up as an explanation of what could have made the investigator sick. Just after a few minutes in there, I began to get a headache as well.

Other than this incident, the night was relatively quiet. Nothing seemed out of the ordinary, and we had not experienced any sounds or equipment readings that were out of the ordinary. We brought Jessica back in the house and continued our investigation for another hour or so with little or no results. As we packed up, I met with the team members outside and we all felt a little disappointed. It didn't feel as we had wasted our time, but we were hoping that with such an active location we would get more activity than we did.

We thanked them for giving us the opportunity to come out and offer an explanation and let them know we would be in touch after a review. As we walked to the cars, I could see the disappointment in my investigator's faces. It had been a long night, and we now had a ton of data to go through.

It didn't take long to get around to the review. The first thing I did was look up information on the house and the property around it. The neighborhood was fairly new, and the house was less than 2 years old. Not much historic information could be found on the land, but the whole area is close to where famous civil war battles took place. After collecting that information, I sat down and popped the tape in from the camera that was in the room over the garage. Hours went by. I saw the upstairs investigators move from room to room, and up to the point where the investigator got sick and went downstairs. Most of the footage was just monotonous but provided good audio and visual of what was going on upstairs. On the last tape, about halfway through, something amazing happened. Right next to the camera, a loud clicking noise, followed by heavy breathing appeared on the audio. The camera had been pointed at the door the whole time, so no one had come in or out of the room for over two hours. Just as the breathing got to the heaviest point, the tripod shook violently and the camera shut off. Watching the video as this happened sent chills down my spine. This seemed impossible. I immediately called the investigators and told them what I had seen. I then ripped the video to the computer and emailed it to all of the team members. No one had seen anything like this.

When I calmed down, I decided to go through the audio. During the entire first hour, while my investigators were upstairs, the longest and strangest EVPs turned up on the audio recorders. For over an hour, you could hear children talking. It sounded like two children having a conversation with each other, and playing games. You could hear them asking for MOMMY, saying they could "Hear the investigators talking, but couldn't see them", you could hear them laughing, it was amazing and heartbreaking at the same time. At no location have I ever captured EVPs that lasted as long in duration as these. At times, the kids would be talking for over two minutes straight. When the talking stopped for the final time, you can hear the investigator in another room say he is feeling sick, and heads downstairs.

Some might say we were picking up the sounds of kids playing outside, but this was well after midnight, and there were no kids outside in the neighborhood. Especially kids that were the age these kids sounded. The truly odd thing is, these voices were captured on the audio recorder placed in the room over the garage where the camera had been physically manipulated. The recorder was less than four feet away from the camera. I synched up the audio from the recorder and the camera, and the sound of the children talking did NOT pick up on the camera's microphone. How is that possible? They were so close together, and both devices picked up the talking of our investigators in other rooms, yet side by side, they did not pick up the same audio of the children. It was very strange. There were no photos taken of significance that night, and nothing else captured on video. The audio was mind blowing.

The next day I made the call to the client and arranged to meet up with them and bring the findings to their house. When Phyllis saw the footage of the tripod being shaken and the camera switched off she immediately jumped up out of her seat. She explained how this was the same thing that had happened to her when they left a camera running to try and capture stuff on their own. While her story did not validate our find, our find was validation for her that it had happened again. Next we played the audio. It got very emotional in the room. The sounds of the children at play, perhaps trapped or lost, brought tears to the client's eyes. At times, the conversation being held by the kids, seemed to acknowledge the investigators in the house. This makes one want to believe that the kids could see and hear us even though we couldn't see or hear them. This was a very emotional case, and for everyone involved it has been one that has stuck with us since.

While I had no explanation of why they were experiencing the activity, it didn't seem to be connected to the daughter. It just seemed that she noticed it more. There is no history, or reason or rhyme that would lead us to believe that the sounds of the children had anything to do with the house or its inhabitants. At most, it could be something tied to the land, but we were unable to find anything of significance to tie it together. For whatever reason, there ARE children there. We heard them on our audio. We can only hope that now we have helped get them noticed, they can get the closure they need to move on.

THE MACO LIGHT

The Maco Light is one of the most talked about ghost stories in North Carolina. I touched on the history of this legend early on, but I did actually investigate and research this phenomenon extensively.

Almost every ghost book that has ever been written on North Carolina, and some national books like those published by Dr. Hans Holzer, have told the stories of the Maco Light for years. Growing up, it was the one thing my father had always said was his only time ever witnessing something supernatural. Thousands of people have witnessed this light. The military had even shut the area down to try and research it. People speculated that it could be headlights from passing cars on the highway, but the reports of this light were around long before the first automobiles made their way into the area. Some have said it could be swamp gas, or the natural phenomena called "Will-O-The-Wisp" (ghostly lights seen at night time near bogs, marshes, and swamps). Granted the old tracks used to run alongside a swamp, so this sounded like it could be a rational explanation, yet the behavior of the light did not match with other known spook lights.

Claims of people seeing the light died out in 1977 when the tracks were removed. This was pretty much the last time anyone had reported seeing it, but then again, times had changed and many people just weren't interested in spending their weekend nights sitting out looking for it. A few investigators have reported other strange findings there in the last few years, but no one has actually been able to capture the light on video.

A few years ago, a friend and I set out to do our own research on the light. We went to the location where the tracks used to lie and set out to explore the area. Quick warning to those reading, most of the area is private property and you never know who you might run into. The land has been sectioned off differently since those days, and simply walking along the old track bed can lead you right into someone's back yard. At the time we went, a school called the Bacon Academy was being built. The main part of the track bed where people said the light would illuminate from was directly behind where this school was being built. We approached the property and sought out the office. We spoke with a few workers who gave us permission to cut through the property and get to the old track bed. It was a beautiful Sunday afternoon, and we were not there to catch a ghost. We just wanted to take pictures for reference during the research. We fired off about a hundred photos and then made our way home.

I loaded the pictures onto my computer and began to flip through them. For the most part nothing stood out. There were some great shots of where the track used to be, and the almost perfectly carved oval through the tree line to make room for the trains that used to come through the area. I got to one photo where a noticed what looked like a gray blob in the background. As I zoomed in on the photo, I could not believe what I saw. It was a figure of an 1800's train conductor! I am usually weary of seeing things in pictures as we have all been victim to pareidolia, commonly referred to as matrixing, and what I saw in this photo was odd. It appeared to be a train conductor, wearing a hat, and black jacket. It was almost too perfect. You could see the shoulder and arms as it overlapped some of the bushes in the foreground, and even though it was overlapping, it was completely see through. What confused me the most was, he had a head.

The local legend claimed a train conductor named Joe Baldwin was decapitated in the train collision and the whole reason for the light was his swinging his lantern while he searched for his head. So why did my guy in the photograph have a head? It was time to do some serious research and get the facts. It was time to separate the legend from the truth.

I visited our local public library, which by the way has its own claims of being haunted, and I immediately went to the North Carolina room and pulled up all of the information on the Atlantic Coast Line Railroad and former employees. An extensive search did not turn up the name Joe Baldwin. Being that the railroad was union, I searched union records to see what would turn up. I did find a Joe Baldwin, but he was killed in action during the battle at Gettysburg and was buried in Virginia, so this wasn't our guy. I started another search. This time I looked for reported accidents resulting in death to an employee for the railroad. This is where it began to get interesting. Ten years before the legend of Joe

Baldwin first saw the light of day, a train accident, in Maco, really did happen. Charles Baldwin, an employee of the Atlantic Coast Line Railroad, was involved in the accident. Just as the story stated, Charles Baldwin had stayed behind in the caboose after uncoupling from the rest of the train. The train pulled ahead into the station for repairs, and then was to come back and reconnect. For whatever reason Charles Baldwin could not get his lantern lit, the report said it was due to humidity, and the trained slammed into him, tossing him from the caboose. According to the coroner report, he died three days later from injuries sustained to the head.

With light of this new information, the photo now made sense. It was also clear that an urban legend had been born from an actual incident. My search for the Maco Light had led me to all of this information that had disproven the legend, and now had gotten me closer to the truth. No one had seen the light for years, yet on a random Sunday afternoon I get a strange apparition in a photo that sent me spiraling into a research frenzy. I felt a breakthrough. I felt like as if the spirit of Charles Baldwin wanted someone to know the truth. Charles, finally someone listened to you. As much as I would like to one day see the actual Maco Light, I am satisfied with my experience during the research of it, and making more sense of a story that had been passed down from generation to generation.

HIDDEN GEM

A fellow investigator and I decided to embark on a serious road trip for a project we were working on. This trip would lead us halfway across the country from North Carolina to Texas.

Prior to us leaving, I had made several phone calls to bed and breakfast houses along our route, to see if we could find anything interesting. Our first stop would be in Alabama in a small town called Vincent, just under an hour away from Birmingham.

We stumbled upon a magnificent find, an old barn that had been moved to a new location, board by board, called Blue Spring Manor. Driving up to this location, it was surrounded by trees, the greenest grass you have ever seen, and looked like something out of a scenery calendar. It still had its original shape, and you could tell it was a barn at one point in time. Before moving, each piece of lumber was numbered and the barn was put in this new location piece by piece in the exact original state. It now sat on what used to be an old horse path.

Lots of new amenities had been added to this property. It had a small pool which doubled as a hot tub, a full service spa, and a small restaurant area that served absolutely delicious food. As we approached the door, we were greeted by some of the staff, and escorted into the main area. A huge fireplace took the center stage. They had a full selection of local wines from a vineyard not far down the road. The overall feeling was very warm and cozy.

We met up with the owner and spoke to her about the property. This place had never been known for having any paranormal activity before, and no teams had ever conducted investigations on the property until the weekend before our arrival. She spoke with us at length about the different experiences she had started to encounter, and what had led up to being interested in an investigation. She took us on a general tour of the location and before showing us to our rooms, made one last stop in the attic.

This particular investigator and I had only been working together for a short period of time at this point. While I am more of a scientific minded person, this investigator has a special gift.

She is very involved in the metaphysical side of things, and definitely has the abilities commonly seen in mediums and psychics. My choice to work with her on investigations has a lot to do with the work of Dr. Hans Holzer, who often used mediums during his research.

After stepping into the attic, she was immediately drawn to a specific corner. I noted this, and we concluded the tour. Shortly after our arrival, it began to rain and a very brief thunderstorm came on. We got settled in our rooms, and then regrouped to start investigating. Armed with cameras, both still and video, radio frequency detectors, EMF detectors, audio recorders, and common sense, we began to conduct our research.

As with any investigation, it was off to a slow start. Some of the rooms throughout the establishment gave various readings on the equipment, but nothing substantial. As we came to one of the main rooms, we settled down to conduct an EVP session. We placed a K2 meter on top of a wooden trunk in the middle of the room, and she began audio while I swept the room for EMF sources. There was a circuit breaker box on the far wall of the room, and just as I suspected, it would bury the needles on the equipment if you came within 3 feet of it. An old style jukebox was on the left wall, and atop that was a picture frame with bronzed baby shoes. Surprisingly, the jukebox did not give off any readings but the bronze shoes seemed to put off a significant amount. The K2 meter on the trunk lay dormant. For over an hour, it sat there with no response or reading.

About halfway through her audio session, we noticed a blip on the K2 meter. A low level frequency had made two of the lights comes on. I immediately opened the trunk to see if anything inside would cause it to go off. Under a layer of blankets and linens was a small metal case and some envelopes. Clearing the trunk out, there were no more readings, but then as it got closer, we realized it was the small metal box giving off the reading. We went downstairs to seek out the owner to find out if it was okay for us to open the box. She came back up to the room with us, and opened the box.

Inside there were funeral notices and pictures of a deceased family member. They had been placed inside this trunk and forgotten about. The owner remained with us while we continued the audio session. During some of the questions being asked, the K2 meter would light up as if in response to the questions being asked by the investigator. The most curious one, was when she asked if the person communicating with us, was the person she felt was in the corner of the attic. At this point, all of the EMF detectors spiked for a duration longer than I have ever seen, as well as the radio frequency detector began beeping. This continued on for a few minutes before the interaction seemed to stop. A few minutes after everything had been quiet, I distinctly heard footsteps in the next room over. I began walking over to where I heard the noise, and right next to my ear, I heard a woman's voice moan.

I had a video camera with me, filming the entire time. I brought the camera back over into the area where my investigator and the owner were sitting, and I played back the video. The sound of the woman moaning had been captured on the camera. As I got up to start walking back out of the room, I felt as if I had stepped into a large spider web and got tangled. It was a light tingling sensation around my arms and neck. We verified that there were no spider webs, and took note.

As the night went on, we did not experience much else. Once everyone had gone to sleep, you could hear the faint sounds of talking throughout the hallways, and even sounds of what could be perceived as furniture or other objects moving.

In the morning, we awoke and headed downstairs. We were greeted with an amazing layout of breakfast. We knew we had to get back on the road but we decided to spend a little extra time at this place because it really was a rare find. I suggest that anyone who is ever in the area, spend the night at this location. If not for the paranormal, then just for the laid back atmosphere.

THE MYRTLES PLANTATION

This location had been on my bucket list for what seemed like an eternity. When you hear tales of Louisiana, you think about voodoo and vampires, slavery, and an abundance of haunted locations. The Myrtles Plantation house is full of history. Originally called Laurel Grove, the house was built by General David Bradford in 1796. Bradford's daughter, Sara Mathilda married Clark Woodruff in 1817 and they had three children; Cornelia Gale, James, and Mary Octavia. Legend has it that they owned a slave known by the name of Chloe.

The story of Chloe is a curious one. She was a slave, whom unlike others, was kept in the house. This was rare for the time. Chloe was caught eavesdropping on a business discussion between Clark and his affiliates and as punishment one of her ears was cut off. In fear of being punished more, or possibly sent out of the house, Chloe plotted her retaliation. She crushed oleander leaves, which are poisonous, and baked them into a birthday cake. Her intentions were to add enough to make the children sick, then nurse them back to health to get back into the good graces of the house, however she apparently added too much. Sara and her two daughters ate the cake and became deathly ill, eventually passing away. Chloe was then hanged as punishment. Some say she was thrown into the Mississippi River, others say she was buried in an unmarked grave. This has become the popular tale at this location. Photos of a ghostly woman have been captured that bear a resemblance to what people think Chloe may have looked like.

In my research, I could not find any historical facts on a slave named Chloe, however, according to the records, Mary Octavia lived for many years while Sara, James, and Cornelia actually fell victim to yellow fever. They died in the same year, but months apart from each other. Some stories also report that Sara and two of the children died in a house fire, but no records support that either. While I am well aware that many facts, such as documented slave ownership, and sometimes even causes of death, were not properly kept in record books, so it is not entirely unlikely that this story is true, however the historical facts would show otherwise.

After the death of most of the Bradford family, the antebellum house was purchased by Ruffin Gray Stirling, who in his passing left the home to his wife, Mary Catherine Cobb. In 1865, Mary hired William Winter as plantation manager and lawyer. Winter went on to marry Mary's daughter, Sara Stirling. They had six children together.

One night, a strange unidentified man rode up to the house. He began screaming and yelling from outside, demanding William to come outside. Mr. Winters exited out onto the porch and was immediately shot. The man rode off. According to house legend, William made his way back into the house and attempted to climb the stairs. He reached the seventeenth step before collapsing and passing away. Other stories say he died there on the front porch and was actually taken away by ambulance, having never stepped foot back into the house. Stories have reported that the man who shot Mr. Winters was E.S. Webber, although no one knows the motive of why it happened. William Winter is the only verified murder that ever took place at the Myrtles Plantation.

It was dark when we pulled up to the house. When we first arrived, I was actually kind of shocked at just how close this house was to the highway. I had always pictured it being deep in the bayous of St. Francisville. Coming down the drive, trees loomed and lurked. It looked exactly like something you would see in the beginning of a horror film. As we came around the way, the house came into sight. I was extremely excited to be there. We parked the car and met with the night time caretaker, Moses. As we stepped into the courtyard, which surrounded a fountain, there were two younger girls outside smoking cigarettes. We spoke to them and found out it was one of their birthdays, and they had decided to spend it overnight in the house.

We went to our room and sat our stuff down. After getting settled, we gathered some equipment and decided to do a quick walk-through of the location. There was no real eerie feeling, and the place seemed to give off a very calm vibe. The two girls from earlier were in a different part of the house, in the upstairs. They joined us as we scouted the area. First we went into the area of the staircase that Mr. Winters had been said to climb. This area also contained a mirror that had become infamous for producing photos of faces. As I inspected the mirror, we were quickly able to determine that oils from fingers and other things had caused the silver plating under the glass to tarnish. We had been told that no matter how many times they cleaned the glass, these spots would never come out. These tarnished marks were actually beneath the glass, and creating the illusion of faces and other shapes on the surface, especially when taking a picture with a camera while using a flash. It did appear that there was a logical explanation for the reports of the mirror, so we proceeded on.

Equipment was placed in various spots throughout the area and we conducted an EVP session. After a few moments, we made our way up the stairs and towards the room where the girls were spending the night. On the nightstand, one of the girls had her laptop and web camera set up to record while they were not in the room. It was set to record using motion detection, so it only recorded small clips at a time when it sensed movement. To their surprise, a few recordings had been made. As they played them back, we watched as it appeared that something was causing draperies on the bed to move. For a moment, we all took a deep breath. My investigator walked over to the area that had been recorded and immediately noticed that the air conditioning vent was pointed directly at the bed. When it would kick on, the draperies would move, thus causing the camera to start recording.

We decided to leave the main house and explore the grounds a little. It was extremely dark and very hard to see. We made our way across a small bridge over a pond and to the gazebo. There have been reports of people seeing civil war soldiers near this gazebo. The night time air was cool, and the night was littered with the sound of bullfrogs and other wildlife. As we began to walk back to the main house, I noticed a light on inside the slave quarters. There appeared to be a shadow walking back and forth in front of a window, but it was only there for a few seconds and never came back. We continued walking towards the courtyard. After a few steps, my investigator spotted something and tried to alert us to what was going on, but couldn't get the words out of her mouth. What she had seen was the figure of a man walking up the staircase in the area where we were earlier. In the excitement, we hurried our way back to that part of the house. One of the girls, who had the key for the door, was shaking so bad she could barely get the key into the lock. Once she got the door open, we frantically tried to search around. No one was to be found. We were the only four people in the house. We sat on the staircase for awhile, waiting to see if anything would happen again. We set up equipment and let it record for the rest of the night while we slept.

In the morning, we awoke and headed down for breakfast. Moses cooks a mean southern breakfast, complete with eggs, biscuits and gravy, and pastries to die for. We interviewed some of the workers at the location to hear some of their stories and personal experiences before we hit the road again. It was an exceptional location, and the history alone was enough to keep me intrigued. Just about everyone who has set foot on that location has had an experience of some sort. I thought that if I was ever going to see a ghost face to face, it would be at the Myrtles Plantation, but alas, even though I experienced some things there, I did not see a ghost.

After I was able to get everything settled and review the footage and audio from the location, there were some peculiar things that happened that we were not aware of at the time. We managed to capture two EVPs on the video camera. Both male voices and both in the same general area. When we did our first EVP session near the staircase, a man's voice clearly said "free beer." For the longest time, I thought maybe this EVP had to do with the fact that the girls were celebrating a birthday party, and indeed there was a cooler of beer just outside the door. After doing some research, I found out that General Bradford was part of the Whiskey Rebellion which came from an excise tax on whiskey in the 1790's. The tax was extremely unpopular with farmers and plantation owners, and usually when being protested, was treated with violence. While it may not be the case, it was definitely an interesting fact to learn after capturing that particular phrase. The other EVP was right after my investigator had seen the man on the staircase. In trying to find if anyone else was in the house, as we entered the room where the girls were staying, one of them called out asking, "Moses, is that you?". The EVP reply was "Could Be." Moses was nowhere near the main house. He was actually in a different building all together and there was no way it could have been Moses voice on the camera. The only other male present, was myself, and it is not even close to sounding like my voice. This is the problem I have with EVPs. We know they are there. We can hear them. People have been collecting EVPs for over eighty years, but we are still unable to prove the source of where they are coming from. For now, we will just have to say that it was a voice that shouldn't have been there, and captured on a night at a location that was primed to be haunted.

GHOSTS OF THE COTTON EXCHANGE

Right in the middle of downtown Wilmington, North Carolina is a honeycomb of shops called The Cotton Exchange. Inside this treasure trove, is a series of stores and restaurants that seem to go on forever. There is a little something for everyone. The Cotton Exchange consists of a combination of several different buildings from downtown Wilmington, in an effort to preserve several historic buildings all at once. Many reports of paranormal activity have stemmed from this small network of shops.

I received a call one evening from the owner of The Top Toad, Diane. She had been experiencing different levels of activity over the course of the last couple of years, and it was beginning to get worse. It started out with objects being moved around, hearing noises, and having the feeling that something was always watching the employees. Every morning she would come in to open up the store and one of the signs that hung from the ceiling would be on the floor. They tried nailing the sign in different positions and reinforcing the sign to make it sturdy, but each morning would be the same result.

The biggest thing she had experienced was a full body apparition of a man dressed in all black with a top hat and cane. On the ground level of the building entranceway, there is a painting of some men dressed in period clothing that were very similar to what Diane was describing. I made note of this painting for my own reference just in case we could possibly tie what she saw to her subconscious knowledge of the painting.

After speaking with Diane at length, she informed me that other shop owners throughout the complex were also experiencing things, particularly a small ice cream shop called The Scoop. After gathering all of the notes on the initial interview with Diane, I made my way across the courtyard to The Scoop and spoke with owners Jef and Deborah. The type of experiences they were having sounded to be above average. They had seen apparitions of a little girl, reflections in the glass around the shop, and even physical manipulation to items in the shop. Jef spoke of a time where he came in to work one morning and saw everything covered in a thick red substance. His initial reaction was panic as he suspected that it was blood. As he got closer he realized it was strawberry syrup. According to his story, it looked as if someone had come in and squeezed an entire bottle all over his counter tops.

All of these stories got me pretty excited. I spoke with a few other shop owners, then held a meeting with my team. I went over all of the stories and reports, and we began to form a plan of attack on how we wanted to investigate this location. We settled on a date and time, and began our pre-investigation research.

Upon arriving on the night of the investigation, we met with Diane who opened the gate for us. It was after business hours and the entire location was deserted. After we got in and set up, Diane locked the steel gate so that we would not be disturbed by anyone. We had control of the environment which is one of the most important things in any investigation. We set up the base camp inside of The Scoop. It was small enough to hold all of our equipment, and still allow us room to move in and out. After getting set up, we were joined by Jef and Deborah who wanted to tag along.

In our typical tradition, we split into two teams. My team started in The Scoop and Team B started in the Top Toad which was in a different building. During the first session, not much seemed to happen at first. While sitting down in the booth with Will, the team documentarian, I had a small digital audio recorder with headphones plugged in that would let me listen to the audio in real time. I asked a few questions, but never heard a response through the headphones. As I started to ask my last question, I felt something tug on the headphone cord and yank it almost a foot and a half to the left. I asked Will if he had touched the cord and he said no, so I immediately asked for it to happen again. Nothing else happened.

I met up with Team B who told me they had a few strange noises and some camera anomalies during their session. Team B entered into The Scoop and my team headed for the Top Toad. Walking into the Top Toad, the first thing I noticed is that there were many reflective surfaces. We had to be careful not to cause false positives on the video. Within a few minutes, we heard what sounded like an iron gate creaking. After checking the gate downstairs, we were able to disqualify it as the object making the noise, and we continued on.

I placed my video camera pointed down one of the aisles towards the back of the store. I had set it on the right hand side, and once positioned, I noticed a t-shirt on the shelf was blocking the view. As I picked up the camera to move it to the shelf on the left side, I saw something flicker in the video. It looked as if a lantern was being lit. It moved across the screen for a second and then fizzled out. I scratched my head trying to figure out what could have caused it. It didn't look natural and there was no reason for the light to be there in the first place. I went towards where it had been seen, and searched the area. I could find nothing that seemed to contribute to the phenomena. As we continued to investigate the store, I split the members of Team A up and we covered the entire store with hand held cameras. As I began to walk down one of the aisles, I heard what sounded like a scraping sound. It started soft and then grew louder. I saw something whip by my camera and then felt a thump on my foot. I took the camera away from my face and looked down. At my feet was a silk flower inside of a small flower pot. I called out to my team and verified that there was no one in the same area as me. I stopped the tape and hit rewind. When I played the tape back, I saw the flower pot move on its own and launch at me. This was my first real experience with object manipulation in a projectile manner.

We went into several of the other stores throughout the Cotton Exchange. There was a Christmas themed store, in which an earlier report said that a lady had a candle thrown at her. It supposedly flew off of a shelf from about nine feet away and struck her in the elbow hard enough to leave a bruise. I was unable to verify this story as more than just someone's personal experience, but the fact that I had a small flower pot thrown at me in the same manner in an adjacent store proved to be quite interesting. As we were leaving that store and heading to an unoccupied space, the door slammed shut on its own, striking Chad in the arm. Again we tried to make it happen a second time, but had no luck.

When we got into the vacant store space, Jef and Deborah from The Scoop joined us. We all formed a large circle around the room. We had several cameras rolling, digital thermometers, EMF detectors, and audio recorders all going at the same time. We all took turns asking questions and trying to get a response. In the video, we had some strange light anomalies, but nothing that seemed too out of the ordinary.

After a long night of investigating, we packed up and

headed home. Over the course of the next two weeks we went over all of the collected data. We had a couple of hits on the audio that we needed to bring back to the Cotton Exchange, along with some photos, and video clips of the strange lantern-like light witnessed in the Top Toad. Most of the EVP came from The Scoop, and only one particular stood out to me. It sounded like a child throwing a temper tantrum and screaming, "I want my ice cream". I found this to be a relevant EVP considering where it was captured. The Scoop was formerly a feed and seed warehouse, and had only become an ice cream shop in the last few years. It seemed as if whatever caused that voice was aware of the business being conducted there. Given the report from Jef of coming into the store and finding the red syrup everywhere, and now hearing this EVP, could it mean that there was a child at play here?

The Scoop was very pleased with the evidence we were able to provide, and they were sure that it was not contaminated, as they were there with us for most of the night. Next we headed over to the Top Toad and presented Diane with the findings. While we did not capture a man in a black coat and top hat, we did have the strange flickering light, and the video of the flower pot being thrown at my feet. Diane did not look shocked. She explained to us that she has always known something was there, and she was happy we were able to capture some of the strange activity that her and her staff had experienced.

Over the course of the next three years, we continued to research and investigate locations inside of the Cotton Exchange. The best way to get an idea of what is happening at a location is to monitor it over time. While one night may be extremely active, it could lie dormant for the next six months. With that being the case, can you really label it as a hot spot? I can without a doubt say that there are a few places in the Cotton Exchange that seem to be active. The Top Toad, The Scoop, the vacant store (first retail space on the left hand side if you enter the door closest to the main building), Paddy's Hollow, and the German Café.

Although I did not talk much about Paddy's Hollow and the German Café in this chapter, the locations did yield a few EVPs and EMF fluctuations. I would need to conduct more research on those locations to come up with answers for some of the unanswered questions we have. The Scoop has been very friendly to us, and has allowed us to investigate many times, so we have more complete data for their location than any other spot in the Cotton Exchange. I will say this, if you are looking to have an experience there, you WILL.

SHE STILL CRIES AT NIGHT

This case was a rather peculiar one. In the paranormal field, we call it striking gold. Not in the sense of it being related to money, but in the sense of, you think you are going into something small, and it turns out to be bigger than you can imagine. This case became so intense, and the activity level of this house is so consistent, that we actually train most of our new investigators at this location. I cannot thank the homeowners enough for the opportunities they have provided for my North Carolina branch team.

A few years ago, our case manager put an ad on a website letting people know that we were offering free investigations. Our investigations have always been free. It is unethical to charge for this type of service, and it is highly frowned upon in the paranormal community. We got an email from a gentleman by the name of Matt, who lived in Burgaw, North Carolina. Matt had been experiencing things around his house, and now that his young daughter had started witnessing it as well, he decided he wanted someone to come and check it out.

As I listened to what Matt had to say, what surprised me the most is that none of his claims seemed exaggerated. His stories never wavered and he remained calm during the conversation. When my team arrived, we took a look at the small three bedroom house, sitting in a cozy nook on a quiet street, and tried to plan out how we would tackle the location.

We broke up into two groups as usual. The square footage on this house was not very large, but it was definitely big enough to have two to three investigators inside at a time. During the first session, I entered with two other team members and we set up a base camp in the living room. We placed all of the equipment in a spread out on the table, and placed all the cases and spare batteries and other equipment in the kitchen area. We began our initial sweep of the house, measuring baseline readings of electromagnetic fields and radio frequencies. We then did a temperature sweep, followed by a still photograph sweep of each room. I also used a noise level meter to determine the baseline decibels of ambient noise in the house. This provides useful when using it in conjunction with a digital audio recorder. A blip on the noise meter may indicate a response that we cannot hear with our own ears, so during EVP sessions, we monitor this as we record.

After we completed an EVP session in the main living room area, we split into different rooms. I had one investigator stay in the living room and the other go into the main bedroom where the clients slept. I took a hand held digital 8 video camera and went into the room where Matt's daughter sleeps. I sat down on the bed and began to pan around the room. On the bed next to me was a baby doll that played music and made noise. Matt and his wife claimed this doll would randomly turn off and on by itself, so I aimed my focus on trying to make the doll turn on by itself. I could hear my female investigator in the living room conducting another audio session, so as not to interfere, I stayed silent. After a few moments, I began to feel a slight chill to the air. There was a sense of uneasiness and I felt as if though something was behind me. I panned the camera over to the closet. Inside the closet was a Sterilite toy bin. In the bin was a small blanket, with the corner hanging off the edge of the bin. On top of the blanket, there had to be about twenty five pounds of toys stacked on it. I panned from the closet to the other side of the room, and just before leaving the room, I panned back over to the closet.

I stepped out of the room and walked into the living room. I mentioned to my investigator that I had a very uneasy feeling and needed to leave that room. She remained in the living room and I made my way down the hall to the client's bedroom.

Upon review of the video tape from the little girl's room, I was in shock at what I saw. As I first panned to the closet, the blanket, on its own, moved as if something had tugged it. I did not see this when it happened, and it happened so fast, that it was easy to miss. As my camera panned to the other side of the room and then back to the closet, the blanket had changed positions and was pulled almost all the way out of the bin to where the corner was now almost touching the floor. I have no explanation of what could have pulled it with such force, but it would have taken a good deal of strength to move the blanket that far. Not only did it move a great deal, but it had done so silently, and did not disturb or move any of the toys that were piled on top of it.

At the time, not knowing what I had captured, I was now standing in the client's bedroom with Chad, my teams's tech manager. He was sitting on the floor with his back to the wall, so I moved to the other side of the room and kept my camera pointed at him. We shouted to the investigator in the living room to let her know that we were going to conduct an EVP session and to stay as quiet as possible. She joined us in the room, and we all settled in.

It was relatively quiet during most of the session. The occasional car would drive by, or a dog would bark in the distance, but nothing to really make note of. Then suddenly, it happened. We heard what sounded like a woman crying. It lasted for a few seconds, then went completely silent. Not sure what we were hearing, Chad and I headed out into the yard. I checked around the house to make sure it wasn't a neighbor, or person walking by, and Chad went under a small opening under the house to make sure it wasn't pipes or an animal.

We came back into the house and went back to the room. We started another session and after a short time, we began to hear the sound of a woman crying again. It was followed by moaning, and what appeared to be sobbing. After a few seconds, it was gone again. We then heard a noise in the adjacent room. We picked up our equipment and made our way over there. We did not hear the sound of the woman again for the rest of the night.

In the next room, which at the current time was being used

for an office, we encountered a radio frequency, but determined it to be the router connected to the computer. Several times while in that room, we all thought we heard what sounded like a male voice. After about half an hour, I saw Chad perk up. He had seen something move through the hallway. A dark shadow, as if a person had just walked through. He jumped up and darted towards it. We followed behind him, but nothing was to be found. We were all alone in the house. He mentioned that he saw it go into the little girl's room, then disappear. We ended our session and Team B entered the house. During their time in the house, they noted a moving shadow in the living room, and hearing what sounded like a man's voice speaking several times.

We ended our investigation for the night, and went home. In the subsequent weeks, we spent a lot of time going through the massive amount of data we collected. There seemed to be so many things, that it was as if we had found a paranormal treasure chest. Several EVPs, strange videos, and a very disturbing picture. I contacted Matt personally to deliver the news and set up a time to meet back with him at his home to show him everything we had gathered.

I started off by showing him the video of the blanket

moving. He was very intrigued, and his wife could not believe her eyes. We also cued up the video of the shadows we caught moving about the house, and at this point I could see Matt start to get nervous. He began biting his nails. I took a moment to explain to him that while these things cannot be explained, it does not mean they are evil, or even there to harm him. Next I showed him the photo that we had caught with the infrared camera. During the investigation, in his daughter's room, I had taken video panning across the bed. As I panned across, there seemed to be something sitting on the bed. I saved it as a still frame and began to try to explain to Matt what the photo was of. In the photo, you can clearly see the bed and the headboard, but as I pan across, there is a black figure, that looked like a small child, sitting on the bed. The top of the head was breaking the line of the headboard and you could plainly see that this object was taller than the height of the headboard. Matt let a deep sigh and began to chew violently on his fingernails. I could tell he was becoming more tense. We then played the EVPs that we had captured. The first EVP was of a male voice saying "Matthew". This was followed by an EVP of the same voice, saying Matthew's name twice in a row. Matt sat with a puzzled look on his face. We had two other EVPs, which the homeowners prefer not to be made public knowledge. Matt told us he thought he recognized the voice as that of his grandfather. He had just passed away recently, and Matt had some of his grandfather's personal items in the house. He made his wife listen to the EVP, and with a stern voice, Matt said "It's him." The last thing we played for Matt was the disembodied voices we captured. We considered these disembodied and not EVPs because we physically heard these with our own ears at the time they happened. You could clearly hear what sounded like a woman crying. Matt said he had no idea what could be the source of this, and had not had a recent female death in the family, nor had experienced any other phenomena that would lead him to believe a female would be present in the house.

We again reassured Matt that he and his wife had nothing to worry about, and if they felt threatened at any point, they should contact their church to try and have the house blessed. He thanked us for our findings, and told us that this evidence would help him better understand how to approach the things he was experiencing in his home.

I would love to tell you that the story ends here, and that Matt and his wife lived happily ever after, but that's not the case.

In fact, the story gets much deeper. The sounds of the crying woman really had me intrigued and I wanted to find out more about the house itself. I spoke with the local historical society and found out some really interesting facts about the house. I called Matt to tell him what he had found out, and he sounded relieved that I had called. He explained to me that he had sent the EVPs we captured to other members of his family who confirmed that the male voice was indeed, in their opinion, that of his grandfather.

As I spoke with Matt, I hoped the new information I was about to give him would help answer some questions about the house. The original owner of the house was a member of the Johnson family. Mr. Johnson was a mason, and he had built this house, which originally sat on the corner of the road adjacent from the cemetery. Upon his passing, his wife had his monument built for his burial site in a place that could be seen from the bedroom window. In later years, after Mrs. Johnson passed away, the house was moved to the current lot where it sits now. The bedroom that she used to be able to see her husband's grave, was no longer facing the cemetery. I believe this may be the cause for hearing the sound of the woman crying in the bedroom. It would make sense to me that if she is indeed still present in essence, that she is in a room where she can no longer see her husband's grave, and is deeply affected by this. We may never know for sure, but it seems probable.

Throughout the course of the last few years, Matt has had things continue to happen at his house. After having a newborn child, they were hearing voices and laughter through the baby monitor, seeing shadow figures dart around the house, hearing unusual noises and the sounds of conversations when no one was present. We not only have continued an ongoing investigation, but have actually brought our new investigators to train there. Matt has been very accommodating when it comes to his home. Anytime anything happens, he calls us immediately. We have collected so much from his house, and we have been able to conduct various experiments over a long period of time, and because of his willingness, we have probably documented enough activity to justify his home being haunted. The research we have done there, and the amount of time we have spent, has made this one of our most complete studies that we have ever conducted.

THE ANCHORAGE INN

A few years ago I was doing some research about haunted locations just outside of our area. Through a couple of quick searches on the internet, I came across a posting on a message board of a woman looking for help. She was the owner of a bed and breakfast in Beaufort, North Carolina. This particularly struck my interest since Beaufort is best known as the town of Black Beard the Pirate.

Stories of this infamous pirate are just about everywhere you turn in North Carolina. He was probably the most famous pirate of all time. He had a severe mean streak, and eventually was captured. While this case was not related to Black Beard, it was going to be amazing just to be in the same town that he called home. His actual home was only a few blocks away from this location.

I contacted the lady and offered up our services. Being a bed and breakfast, they not only were more than anxious to have us come out, but also would provide rooms for us to sleep overnight in. This would be a great opportunity to be able to investigate throughout the whole night, without having to worry if it was getting too late at night. When we got to the location, the client met us in front and gave us the tour. The house was massive. It was warm and inviting, and had a style of southern charm to it that seemed to be very welcoming. There was a beautiful staircase that led from the main floor up to the second floor where most of the bedrooms were located. As we walked from place to place, she told us of the strange things that have gone on in the house. Nothing seemed to be out of the usual. They would hear the occasional footsteps, voices of people talking when the house was empty, but probably the biggest thing they have experienced there was seeing an apparition of a woman.

After taking notes, we went out to the vehicles to unload the equipment. Before we made it back into the house the client approached us outside. She also owned a yellow Victorian house directly next door. She asked if we had time to check that location as well because they were recently renovating and things were starting to happen in that house as well. We agreed to check it out, and to us, it felt like just an added bonus. After getting all of the equipment set up and establishing a home base, we split up through the house, and I sent Team B over into the Victorian.

My team started in the downstairs bedroom. We kept in contact with the other team via walkie talkies. I am not a fan of having an open radio frequency during the investigation because of its possible effects on the sensitive equipment, but since we now had twice as much ground to cover, we decided to keep our lines of communication open. Within the first thirty minutes, we experienced the first of what would be many activities during the night. I sat on the bed, Key, our case manager, sat in a chair, and Will, the documentarian, stood in the doorway. We were just having a casual talk about how we were planning on making the area sweep when all of a sudden, we heard several loud thuds. It was so loud, it sounded like a pack of elephants went running through the house. I called out over the radio to ask if Team B was out of the house yet, and they confirmed that they were inside the Victorian. They also confirmed that they heard the noise too. Our team not only heard the noise, but we felt it shake the floors and vibrate the walls. Key went to check the main staircase and brought to our attention that it sounded like as if someone had fallen down the stairs. We had a hard drive camera at the bottom of the stairs, so we did an instant review. About thirty four minutes into the footage, you could hear the loud bangs and the camera shook violently as if some invisible force had come down the stairs.

After a few minutes of trying to figure out what could have caused it, and dismissing the idea of water pipes, we decided to press on through the house. We focused on the dining area and the main living area downstairs. After a couple of hours with nothing, we decided to head upstairs. On the third floor, almost immediately, the EMF detector began to go off. I followed it all the way into a particular bedroom, and it got stronger. As I got further in the room, I was able to determine the source of the field. There was an exposed copper wire that ran all along the frame of the window. We sat in the room for a little bit and conducted an EVP session. All of a sudden, we heard what sounded like footsteps just outside the room. Will wheeled around and saw what appeared to be a figure running down the stairs. We all got up and went out into the hallway. You could see what appeared to be the shape of a person, in shadow form, moving up and down the steps. This happened for about six to eight seconds, then was gone.

I again radioed over to Team B to see if they were having anything happen. Other than some strange noises, they weren't really experiencing anything, so after telling them what was happening in the Anchorage Inn, they were anxious to get over here. We switched places, and Team A entered the Victorian.

They were definitely doing work on the house. Much of the floors had been torn up and the walls had been sanded down. There were tools lying around, and there were some rooms that were piled wall to wall with furniture. We decided to set up our equipment, and leave it running while we went outside for about thirty minutes. This would allow us to record everything with as little contamination as possible.

Just across the street was the public library, of course it was closed at this time of night, but directly behind the library was a huge cemetery. We decided to check it out. We didn't attempt to investigate it, but we enjoyed the sights of the iron gates and decades old tombstones. We took some photos and headed back to the Victorian.

Once back, we went inside and did a typical EVP session as

well as walked around with our cameras, trying to collect as much data as possible. I checked in with Team B who was now inside the Anchorage Inn, and it seemed they were experiencing some things on their own. One of the investigators claims that he heard a small voice of a child saying "mama" a few times. The other investigators heard music playing, and heard the sounds of someone running around in the house. This was great to hear. They had experienced the same thing, so they could now validate what we had experienced earlier.

We decided to bring the entire group together for one last EVP session in the main area of the Anchorage Inn. We cleared all of the equipment out of the Victorian and gathering in the living room of the Inn. For over an hour, we continued to take readings as we did our EVP session. During one point, it appeared as if we were getting direct responses. When an investigator would ask a question, we would get a strange response back almost immediately on the equipment. A light would blink if the answer was yes, or a noise would buzz if the answer was no. It could have been totally coincidental, but it only did this for a period of about two minutes before stopping all together.

We now had a ton of stuff to go over. Our single

investigation had turned into a double. We already knew we had things, since most of it happened while we were present in the rooms, and none of it was subtle.

The photos we took turned up to be average. There was nothing in them that would suggest anything of a paranormal nature. Mostly dust and moisture plagued these photos. The video showed that something had either shook the entire house, or had "fallen" down the staircase and bumped into the camera. We still had no explanation of what made this possible. On one of the video cameras placed inside the Victorian, we caught something we did not expect. As we placed the video cameras down, and went to check out the cemetery, shortly after we left you could hear a noise. It sounded like furniture sliding. A few seconds later, you could hear a high pitched squeaking noise. Then we noticed the cabinets in the kitchen area of this old Victorian were opening and closing on their own. They would open slowly causing the squeaking noise, then would slam shut, creating the sound like furniture sliding. I almost could not believe my eyes. I had always heard about this type of phenomena, but had never actually seen it firsthand.

The audio turned up a few EVPs that we were not able to

decipher. Out of five of them, the only one we could tell what was being said, backed up what our investigator heard. We heard what sounded like a child's voice saying "mama."

It seemed that our client was right about her gut feeling of having some strange activity in the Inn and the Victorian. It was definitely something that I had never experienced before up to that point. It didn't seem threatening or harmful. If anything it seemed to have a residual feel to it. A residual style of activity means the same events happen over and over again like a looped video. The theory on that is that it will happen whether you see it or not. It does not know you are there, or even if you can see it. It generally would not be able to interact, and therefore would night be able to harm or hurt anyone. The client seemed satisfied with what we had found, and almost relieved. She was worried that she was imagining all these things, and that the stress of running the bed and breakfast was making her lose her mind. We assured her that is not the case, and to feel free to contact us again if she would ever like us to come back. As with all clients, I suggested she keep a diary of activity, so that we could compare the times, length of activity, and circumstances around her activity. If she would keep up the diary for a year, we may find information that will correlate and possibly help us understand more about her activity.

MERMAID MANOR

Mermaid Manor was a learning experience for me and my team. We got the call to investigate this beach house that was renting the rooms out as a bed and breakfast. I made the first trip to the location and scouted the outside. It was painted in pastel colors and sat directly on the ocean front. It was cozy atmosphere. I spoke with the owner about the different things that had gone on and been reported by the tenants of the building. I learned that one of the women renting a room on a monthly basis and had lived there for almost two years, was a psychic and had a ton of experiences. The stories of this location ranged from hearing footsteps, eerie feelings, disembodied voices, and full body apparitions. There was not a whole lot of history to be found on the place, but this entire beach has a history of civil war battles. It is about two miles away from historic Fort Fisher, so the area is rich in possible stories of hauntings.

I decided to bring the entire team up and conduct a very thorough investigation. None of the tenants would be present, and we would have the entire house to ourselves. On the night of the investigation, we used a DVR system for surveillance purposes. The DVR system consisted of four wired infrared security cameras running to a large hard drive that can record for numerous hours. As it recorded live, it was displayed on a monitor which allowed us to keep a better eye on multiple locations at once. This would be one of the last times we would use a DVR system. While it has its pros and cons, I have found more cons than pros and I will explain this in a later chapter. We set all of our equipment up and decided on a plan of attack. There were two stories to this house, so we had a team on each floor, and one person monitoring the DVR system from the living room lobby area. There were two large French doors that sectioned the lobby off from the rest of the house, so this made for a perfect spot to set up a base camp.

One known story of significance is that a woman died while on the toilet in one of the upstairs bathrooms. Knowing this was the only confirmed documented death, we focused on that room and bathroom with the most equipment.

At almost fifteen minutes into the investigation, strange things started happening right off the bat. We had infrared motion detectors set up in the room that began going off by themselves. We found no viable reason for this to happen. Shortly after that, we began to hear different noises throughout the house. Sounds of feet shuffling in the hallway, and what sounded like a door down the hall opening and shutting by itself. We did a complete inspection but did not see any source of what was causing the noise.

Towards the end of the investigation, we convened in the bedroom of the lady who had passed while using the bathroom. We did a technique known as provoking. We would say certain things related to the time period and possible last moments to try and get a response. "Are you okay in there?", "You have been in the bathroom for a very long time, is everything alright?", "Can you bring us a towel?", etc. During this session we recorded what sounded like a female's voice responding several times on our audio recorders. I thought it was a great catch based on the story.

As we began to pack up, I monitored the DVR system while the other investigators finished up their last sessions and began to pack up the equipment. Just before we started to break down the DVR system, I noticed something on the screen in the hallway near the stairs. I could not believe what I had just seen. I called the other investigators into the room and we played back the footage several times. Everyone was in shock. The owner of the property was there, and when she saw the footage, she became so scared that she refused to stay in the house. What we saw on the camera appeared to be the materialization of an apparition in the full body form of a woman. It started slow, then came into full view and looked as if she quickly darted around the corner. As I looked over the faces of my team mates, I saw some of them on the verge of tears from the excitement. After a brief discussion, we broke down the DVR system and called it a night.

Outside of the location, I spoke with my lead investigator about what we thought we had captured. If this turned out to be what we thought it was, this would be the holy grail of investigations. We would have the best footage of an actual ghost ever recorded. There is a saying, "If it seems too good to be true, then it probably is." This could never have applied more than it did to this footage.

For over a week we analyzed the footage trying to come up with answers. We knew we would have to go back to the location and try to figure this out. At the time this footage was recorded on the DVR, one of my investigators was upstairs with his hand held miniDV camera. We pulled his footage and matched up the time stamps. We scripted out his exact movements based on what his camera was pointed at. We printed this out and returned to the location.

After returning, we set the DVR system and cameras back up to the exact position they were during the investigation. I sent the investigator up to the second floor, and from in front of the DVR system, I read all of his steps back to him and had him walk to exact path he had walked on the video. I called these out to him from a walkie-talkie and I watched the screen steadily. At one point, I called a step out to him, and instantly sank. What we thought was going to be a great video, was now just recreated.

Basically what had happened was, the infrared illuminator on the camera being used by the investigator hit just the perfect angle to create the illusion. When pointed at the corner of a picture frame, it reflected from there to the wall, from the wall to the ceiling, and from the ceiling through a tiny gap in the staircase. What the DVR camera was seeing was the downward beam from the illuminator coming through the gap. What looked like legs was actually part of the staircase railing. It was something that would never have happened if the camera didn't hit the angles just right.

While it was deflating for the morale of the team, it was also a boost. We had done our job. We could now say this is something we could explain. It was very important to us to find an answer before posing this footage as evidence. We didn't put it up on the websites as evidence, or get so far ahead of ourselves in being so confident that it was definitely paranormal. I was proud of the team for being able to recreate it. If we had foolishly presented it as evidence, it would have hurt our credibility as researchers.

Aside from that, we did have the few unexplainable things happen to us during the investigation, so we definitely felt there was activity going on there. We have returned to Mermaid Manor a few times to follow up on experiences. The woman who claimed to be a psychic had moved out shortly after our first visit, and not due to fear, but because she was only there until she found a permanent place to live. Since she has been gone, none of the other tenants, nor the owner, have had experiences or strange things happen. One would have to think of the possibility that whatever was going on there was linked to the psychic, but that's only speculation.

A SOLDIER SPEAKS

It's pretty rare that we get called out to a location that provides phenomenal evidence. Especially when the particular happening seems to possibly be the link to the other side. This next case was one in particular that I felt could have led to some great break-throughs had we been able to get back to the location. This chapter also holds a very important lesson on why you should not allow the homeowners to always be present during an investigation.

This case was referred to us by a previous client. In the process of telling people he knew about the things we found during our time in his home, one of the people he spoke with immediately wanted us to come check out his home. He was an older gentleman, who lived with his mother. They had a double wide trailer on a huge piece of land out in the country. He and his mother had very strong and firm religious beliefs. From the moment we walked in the door, the first things I noticed were the pictures of Jesus, crosses, and other church related objects lining the walls of the home. They were very warm and inviting and in appreciation for us coming out on our own time, his mother had prepared sandwiches, snacks, and even baked cookies for us.

As usual we conducted an interview to try and get a better understanding of the things they experienced in the house. Based on their stories, we began to set up the equipment in various areas throughout the house, and we got settled in. This was one of the first times that we had come across this request. The mother and son insisted that they be present during the investigation. They wanted to see the stuff as it happened. I explained to them that investigating is not like you see on television. Sometimes we sit around in the dark for hours waiting for something to happen, and it can get quite boring. Nonetheless, the wanted to sit in on the investigation, so we obliged.

We had a potential new investigator on this case, and we had brought him along for training. After this night, it would be the last time we saw or heard from him. Nothing much seemed to be happening for the first part of the night, but once in awhile we would hear a shuffle or loud rapping noise coming from the bedroom area. This bedroom happened to be the mother's room. It too was filled with religious artifacts as well as knick-knacks and stuffed animals. We all congregated into that room.

With video cameras running on tripods from four different angles, several audio recorders, motion detectors, and EMF sensors, we began a group session. We attempted to hold an EVP session, but seemed to be getting no direct results. After sitting there in a circle for a short time, the mother began to tell us stories of strange things that had happened to her, and a few strange dreams she had been having as of late. In the middle of her story, a motion detector aimed at the large bathroom kicked on. No one was in the bathroom and no one was in direct sight of the infrared beam to cause it to go off. My first impression was that maybe a neighbor or someone had walked by the window and the detector had been set off by a shadow. I went outside to try and set it off through the window myself. No luck. I came back inside and we continued on.

This time I asked, "Can you give me a sign to let me know that it was you who set off the motion detector?". Just then a loud thump came from upstairs. Everyone looked startled, and I asked, "Was that you who just made the noise in the attic?". Once again, another loud thump rang out. "If that is you, can you come downstairs and make a noise down here?". This time the thump was louder, and it came directly from the bathroom in front of us. The motion detectors went off in time with the thump. I heard the mother gasp for air. "I don't want to do this anymore. Let's please stop". I could tell she was frightened. As I tried to calm her down, her son reminded her that we were here to find answers. He sounded more like he was saying this out loud to try and convince himself though, because we could tell he was getting scared as well. I tried to go a little different direction with the questions. "If you can hear my voice, can you knock once for yes, and twice for no?". A single knock echoed. "Okay, just to be sure can you knock twice if you heard me?". Two knocks. I could see the posture of my team changing as they looked both amazed and unsure at the same time. I went into the bathroom alone, leaving the double French doors open for the team to be able to see the whole room. This was a master bedroom bath, so it was very large. Dead in the center of the bathroom was a large tub and just to the left was a shower stall. I sat on the edge of the tub and asked; "Would you like to communicate with me? One knock for no, and two knocks for yes.". Two knocks.

My next mission was to try and get a name. It was going to be a long and tedious conversation this way, but it seemed to be working. "Okay, I am going to go down the letters of the alphabet. When I say the first letter of your first name, knock for me. I will do the same for the second letter, third letter, and so on. Will you help me figure out your name? One knock for yes, two knocks for no.". One knock. So we began.

At the end of the session we had gotten a name. Abner Johnson. We also had asked if he was in the military because of the civil war ties to the land. The responses indicated that he was involved with the civil war. We ended our session, and shut down the investigation. The mother and son clients were getting extremely ridden with anxiety, and we did not want to subject them to further tension. Before we left, we wanted an immediate result on the name we found. I had never had anything like this happen on a case before, or since. I asked if we could use their computer to access some historical sites and files, and they happily agreed. Within a few minutes, I found what we were looking for. Something that would prove to be truly significant. During the civil war, Abner G. Johnson of the North Carolina Fifth Regiment served in this area. This was not a common name to just come out of the blue. The responses we had gotten through the knocks and bangs had actually spelled out this entire name and occupation as if communicating through a primitive Morse Code.

As we packed up the leave, the unnerved homeowners packed as well. Based on what they had seen and heard, they did not want to stay in the house alone after we left and had made arrangements to stay with family. In my professional opinion, I know they were curious as to what was going to happen during the investigation, but a deeper issue now took place. This was a very rare event, and in no way, shape, or form, did it seem like it had intention to harm anyone. It was a very calm form of activity, but to those not used to activity, it could scare you. I hated to see that they were so scared, and I know that had they not been present during the investigation, they would be sleeping in their own beds. I know deep down that they had nothing to worry about, but trying to convince a person who is that afraid of the unknown is a difficult task. People fear what they don't know.

After going home, we analyzed all of the video and audio. I had a team member transcribe all of the knocks and bangs as an actual conversation. After reading through it, it was as if this entity was just happy to have someone to talk to, and it amazed me that we seemed to have such a great two way conversation. As I did more research on Abner G. Johnson, we were able to trace his name back to the ownership of the actual land that our client's double wide trailer is now sitting on. After the war, the military could not afford to pay Mr. Johnson his promised salary, so he was given these tracts of land to compensate for their shortcomings. Mr. Johnson died shortly after, and the land was passed on to several different families before ending up with the current owners. We were able to find land deeds all the way back to the ones signed by Mr. Johnson himself.

After finding out this new information, I called the son and spoke with him about the findings. They still had not returned to their house and it had been almost four days since our investigation. I offered to return for a follow up investigation and he agreed to have us out the following weekend.

I was excited about this location, and what might come of it. If this entity was able to communicate full sentences as if it understood us, I wanted to know what other things it could tell us. Maybe it could tell us how life after death is. Maybe it would be able to explain what actually happens when we die. The possibilities were endless, and my mind raced with new questions to ask for the next opportunity. Alas, it was short lived.

It was Friday. We were scheduled to return to this home on Saturday evening. I was sitting in a local restaurant having lunch around 1pm, when my phone rang. I looked down and saw it was the client, and answered excitedly. He told me they had gone back to the house and slept there on Thursday night, but were still too scared of the house to stay. He had gone to a member of their church who recommended that they seek their pastor to come in and bless the house. With this news came the crushing blow that our investigation would be cancelled and they were now putting it into the hands of the church. My heart sank. I didn't argue with them or express disappointment. My number one concern was that the clients get the answers they seek. While it was heartbreaking to think that we are missing an incredible opportunity to possibly strike up communication that would lead to the answers being sought after in this field, I thanked them for having us out and told them that we would always be a phone call away. I have not heard from these clients again, so I am assuming their troubles have been taken care of. I often think back to this case and how if we only had one more chance to get back there, maybe, just maybe, we would have learned something.

So this is a good indication of why the homeowners might not need to be present during an investigation. They don't understand the work and they can easily get scared or stressed out for the smallest thing. Would they have reacted the same way if they had just heard about it, but not actually witnessed it? Who knows. We were just grateful to have the opportunity for such a unique case. I still seek cases that are comparable to this one with the communication factor. I may never see another one in my lifetime, but at least I have this one. And for those of you wondering about the investigator we were training that disappeared after this case, needless to say he didn't make the team.

THE METAPHYSICAL STORE

It's not very often that I come across small metaphysical shops in my hometown. These stores sell various things with "healing properties" such as crystals, as well as books, relaxation music, dowsing rods, and things that most people would call New Age. A friend of mine had recently told me about this particular small building and that they have Psychic Fairs on every other Saturday of the month. Letting my curiosity get the best of me, I decided to stop in one day during the week and check the place out.

From the moment I walked in, I was greeted with soothing music playing over the speakers, the smell of burning incense, and a friendly woman behind the counter. She happened to be the owner of the business, so I immediately introduced myself. After a few minutes of back and forth banter, we came to the subject of ghosts. This led to a string of stories about the house now converted to metaphysical shop, and that they, themselves, have been experiencing phenomena. She had a friend who was into the paranormal who came out and took some photos inside the shop, so she pulled them up on the computer to show them to me. I didn't see anything too much out of the ordinary. A few "orbs" which could easily be explained away, and a few photos of a "mist" were at the top of her trophy photos. The mist was something I had doubts about simply for the fact that they burn incense there during hours, and the mist could easily be the smoke from the burning incense. Being that the place is frequented by psychics, it was interesting to hear the stories the psychics provided to this lady. She was told that the business was a portal, and that in the far back room it served as a place for weary spirits to stop and rest. I am not one to buy completely into stories from psychics without some hard evidence to back it up.

After about an hour of talking, she invited my team and I to come back sometime to do an investigation. Since we had never investigated this sort of location before, I agreed, and scheduled a time for us to come back. There was not a whole lot of history on the location at all. It was a former residence that had been zoned to commercial as well as residential, so it was serving the purpose of strictly running as an independent shop.

On the day of the investigation, I gathered a few of the team members. Since this location was rather small, I limited it to only four including myself. I had requested that one of the resident psychics accompany us during this experiment because I wanted to see if we could find any readings or other evidence that would correlate with what the psychic was picking up on. Although she had asked several psychics to participate, none of them agreed. She did have a friend however, who claimed to be sensitive, that agreed to help out the best she could. A sensitive is not too different from psychic, but while they can sense things, they cannot pick up on readings like a psychic would. It was going to be interesting.

In typical fashion we split the group up and conducted individual sessions. I took along my team documentarian, Will, and we headed to the first room. In this room, the sensitive referred to it as the Angel Room. She said that Angels frequently visit that room. In only a few minutes, she burst into tears. Will and I looked at each other confused. He filmed while I took readings with the equipment. She talked about feeling pain, and lots of sorrow. I did not get any strange readings, nor did we pick up anything on the video. A later review of the audio, to our surprise, contained the sound of what sounded like wings flapping. That is the only way I know how to explain the sound. There were a few possibilities of what the noise could have been, but we didn't know for sure so we moved on.

In the main room of the shop, the sensitive stopped and pointed at a wall. This wall was directly behind the stereo unit. She said there was a portal on that wall. While we did get EMF readings, it was due to the electrical wiring from the stereo and the speakers. We kept a video camera recording on the wall for the duration of the night and set up a digital camera on a tripod to take photos of the wall. The video provided no results and there were no anomalies in the photos. I was beginning to have my doubts, not just about the sensitive, but about the building in general having any activity.

We then proceeded to another room which was used mostly for psychics to use while giving their readings. In this room I sat along a wooden bench seat. Will sat in the opposite corner, and the sensitive sat across from me in a wooden chair. She mentioned that she felt the presence of several spirits in the room, but they were shy. They were curious about us, but did not want their presence to be known. I let out a sigh then started to stand up. As I leaned forward to stand, I feel an icy cold breeze rush by my leg. I only felt it on one leg and not the other. I am not fast to call this paranormal, but it was a strange feeling.

We dismissed the sensitive, and Will and I headed to the back corner room where they claim spirits come to rest when passing through. It was a very tiny room, barely big enough for two people. We had a video camera on a tripod in one corner facing a small round table in the center of the room. Will and I both had hand held video cameras, and we sat across from each other at the table. For about the first half hour, we didn't notice anything unusual. The occasional car would pass by on the road outside, but the room was relatively quiet. We decided to conduct an EVP session. During the session we asked for knocks and bangs, and the usual things for an entity to make itself known.

On the table was a small glass vase with colored glass stones inside of it. It also had pens and pencils tucked into it. After one of the questions, we heard the glass slightly make a noise as if it had been bumped. Every once in awhile, I could feel a vibration on the table. I looked underneath to make sure there were no motors or anything, to be sure the table was not rigged for entertainment purposes. It was not. It was just a plain, round, wooden table. I told Will to continue his line of questioning. After each question, the table would shake a little and we could hear the glass stones rattling in the vase. Will and I looked at each other to make sure neither of us were touching the table. We were a good foot and a half away. He filmed me, as I filmed him. The third camera on the tripod filmed both of us. This was perfect coverage to show that neither of us were shaking the table. The shakes began to get harder. They got louder. We decided to get up to leave, as we were both kind of spooked, and as I stood up, the table shot up and smacked me in the thigh. We made our way out of the room and found the rest of the group. We told them what had just happened, and the other two investigators immediately went in. It did not happen again.

After long hours, we wrapped up and concluded the investigation. Our audio and video provided no significant evidence other than the sound of the wings flapping, and of course our experience with the table. Watching it on video in slow motion, I was simply amazed at how the table moved over a foot and lifted off the ground to hit me that high up on my leg. I had never had anything happen to me like that before and it was definitely an experience I would not forget. As for Angels, portals, and the other things, I did not find anything to back up what the sensitive was picking up on so I am not sure what to believe. Maybe we were there at a time when the activity was not in place. The owner claims that because they sell plenty of objects with mystical properties, that the spirits are drawn there. If that is true, then one day I hope to get back there and check it out when the spirit traffic is high.

A METAPHYSICAL EXPERIENCE

One thing as an investigator that I try not to do is forget the roots of what started paranormal investigating. For the longest time, this field was considered very metaphysical, which is based on happenings or activity that is experienced outside of human perception. It is the act of studying things that cannot be discovered or experienced through the process of everyday life. The spirit realm was lumped in with things like religion, and collectively this is what defines the metaphysical study.

Over the course of the last few years, the definition has kind of changed. As ghost hunting became more of a mainstream hobby, it was because of popular television shows claiming to invoke the scientific method that has caused this change. Now, the definition is more angled to people or groups not using scientific methods, and they are referred to as metaphysical groups. My team

Research: Paranormal combines a healthy dose of metaphysical methods into our investigations to make sure we are collecting all possibilities. Most teams these days are using what is referred to as scientific equipment, which I will address in a different chapter, and some new devices for the metaphysical side have began to bleed over.

This particular incident took place in 2009 when I took my team up to a location in New York for an investigation. In previous chapters I have spoke several times about Dr. Hans Holzer. Over the years, since his passing, I have had the privilege of working with his daughter, Alexandra. She and I have grown rather close, and I feel as though she was my own flesh and blood sister. She is a brilliant author and following in her father's footsteps, she is an effective investigator. We arranged for Alexandra to meet us at the location. Her father had passed away in April and the entire paranormal community lost a great asset and huge contributor to the research of the field.

At this location we investigated for nearly a week straight. We slept in shifts and we investigated for twenty four hours a day, taking breaks only to eat and regroup. The first night in the location Alexandra arrived in her usual fashion. She had a glow about her that I can only explain as "it". She looked like a movie star. After being around her for only minutes, you could feel her energy. Again I am not one to usually pick up on these sort of things, since I do not consider myself sensitive, or psychic by any means, but there was definitely something about her that stood out.

After making all of the greetings, we set up to investigate. I am only going to focus on one particular instance of this investigation because still to this day, I am baffled. We investigated for a few hours, then decided to do what we brought Alexandra out for. Something that is hardly ever done on investigations anymore. A séance. Alexandra is a medium, or as she refers to herself, an intuitive. I thought it would be a great idea to have her conduct this séance in metaphysical fashion while we used our scientific techniques to try and capture any evidence of the séance being successful. My team, along with the location's owner, and Alexandra all gathered around the table. The table was lit with candles, and on the table in front of Alexandra was a drinking glass turned upside down. This would be the means of communication. Everyone joined hands and after Alexandra said a few words for protection, and the séance began. With her hands on the glass, Alexandra began to ask for signs of lurking spirits or anyone else who may want to make themselves known by moving the glass in patterns for yes or no. Time after time the glass would move and answer the questions she would ask. During this, we filmed from different cameras as well as had every piece of equipment running that we had on hand. During the session we were not getting any correlating readings, so even though it seemed that something was happening, we had nothing to show for it other than the moving glass.

I then introduced an experimental piece of equipment that is now growing largely in popularity regardless of its questionable results. This device is known as the "ghost box". It's basically an AM/FM radio that has been manipulated to scan through radio frequencies creating a white noise that theoretically will allow a spirit to communicate with an audible voice you can hear through the speakers. For those reading this that have used them before, and for those reading this that are already rolling your eyes, I just want to make this clear. I do NOT put much stock into these devices as I believe that a new series of false positives are introduced with this device, and again I will explain this in another chapter. However, this instance I will have to say is entirely unique. What I am about to tell you really happened, and I have no idea how it was possible.

We ran this ghost box and its annoying sounds of scanning channels for about fifteen minutes. We heard random voices, broken sentences, and non consequential gibberish. Then in an instance a voice spoke over the speaker. I shook my head. I could not believe what I was hearing. I looked directly at Alexandra. We both recognized the voice. It spoke several times, including introducing himself by name, Holzer. Yes, you read that right. As you can imagine, Hans being from Austria had a distinguishable accent. It was undeniably his voice. Alexandra followed up with a series of questions, all answered by the same voice. There is no way that with the constant rolling of the channels that we should be getting one solid voice over a series of channels. He answered questions that no one else in the room knew. He called Alexandra by her nickname that only he knew. He asked about her daughters by name, he mentioned Alexandra's sister, and the conversation lasted nearly twenty five minutes before his voice finally began to fade below the noise. As the room fell silent, it became one of the most emotional experiences I have had on an investigation. Alexandra sunk her head into her hands and burst into tears. My heart sank to see this, and I ran over to console her. The loss of her father was very hard for her, and even though this contact with him proved to her that he was still around, it was still something you can never prepare for emotionally.

Watching the footage later and seeing it as it happened still brings a tear to my eye. This doesn't stop the story though. I was anxious to get home and watch all of the video we shot during this time and hopefully see something that was going on during this session. The first half hour of the video was fine, nothing out of the ordinary. The first time the voice comes through and introduces himself as Holzer, the digital tapes on all of the running cameras seemed to malfunction. It was as if they had some type of magnetic interference. I was getting angry as I was importing the tapes because it had pretty much wiped out the entire conversation. The video was distorted and the audio was nonexistent. Then during the conversation when the voice of Dr. Holzer told Alexandra that he loved her, the tape cleared up. We ran three different video cameras, one Canon and two Sony cameras. The tapes for all three cameras were all messed up in the same spot, and for the same length of time. I cannot simply chalk this up to camera malfunction since it was on multiple cameras. The chances of all three tapes being damaged in the same spot are slim to none. They were different brand tapes, came in separate packages, and were stored in different equipment cases, yet all had the same issue.

I have to chalk this up to a crazy, but very emotional metaphysical experience. We used a device that has not been proven, and when tested has had an accuracy of 0.003 in the experiments we ran, which is well below any acceptable standards in the scientific community. Alexandra and I are both very familiar with her father's voice, she more than I, and that WAS his voice we were hearing. It was not being manipulated by any outside sources since it does not have a function like a walkie-talkie or two way communicator device, and the ghost box was in my hand the entire time of the séance, so I had complete control over the device. Since this investigation Alexandra has had several instances of contact by her father, and I have also had his voice come through for me on one other occasion. No matter how much I believe, and deep in my heart I know it was him, a skeptic would never believe this story, and I would never expect them to. I don't need them to. It was something that meant a lot to me as a follower and pupil of Dr. Holzer, and I know for Alexandra, hearing her father's voice was just what she needed, even if she wasn't ready to hear it.

At the location this took place, we had several other happenings during our time of investigating, but most of them were easily explained away. There were small things here and there, but not enough for me to conclusively decide on the level of activity there. We were there for nearly a week, and I am confident that my team put forth a level of effort they had never done before. It's not to say that this location wasn't active, but there definitely was nothing that kept us from being able to sleep at night, other than our dedication to investigating.

COME FOR THE FOOD, STAY FOR THE GHOSTS

The next few chapters are going to focus on a few places I have had the privilege of investigating in the great state of Texas. It's a state I dreamed of living in as a little kid, I grew up a huge Dallas Cowboys fan, and I am fascinated with the lifestyle of the old west. I am not big on western movies, but I love a good book on gunfighters, pioneers, and gold rush towns. A lot of Texas towns are still original buildings and have that old frontier town feel to them.

This first location, located in Waxahachie, Texas, is known as the Catfish Plantation. I had heard about this restaurant from many investigators and had seen it featured on many shows. When

I found out I was going to have the opportunity to investigate it, I was immediately excited. The location is notorious for having activity every half hour. That is extremely active for a location. Most places only have something happen once a month, some as few as once every couple of years.

About thirty five miles south of Dallas, you will find the small town of Waxahachie. It's a quiet little town with a small downtown city square. Just outside of downtown, you will find Catfish Plantation, a Victorian house built in 1895 that has been converted to a restaurant and is one of the top ten catfish restaurants in Texas. I was attracted there by not only the activity, but the menu. Everything you order at this place is delicious. The owners are a lovely family and they really take care of people. On my first trip down, Shawn, the owner's daughter and head chef introduced me to something that would become my favorite dish, and I have ordered it on every trip I have taken to Waxahachie, sweet potato fries with white chocolate dipping sauce. The amounts of food they serve on the plate are enormous. I usually end up taking over half of it home in a box. Their menu is what has made them coin the term "Come for the food, and stay for the ghosts."

Just like their generous portions of food, they serve up a large order of paranormal activity. Since we have investigated this location and held events there multiple times, I will conduct this chapter as the highlight reel of experiences me and my team have had there. When investigating Catfish Plantation, I am usually accompanied by our team medium, my Dallas case manager Buffy, and fellow investigator Jimmy. Jimmy runs a team that is a sister team to Research: Paranormal, so when I am in the area, we usually invite him out with us, or we accompany him on some of his locations that he has set up.

Some of the reports that have arisen at the location include, employees experiencing object manipulation, full body apparitions, and disembodied voices. The house was the birthplace of Paul Richards, a famous baseball player who played for the New York Yankees. None of the reports seems to be related to him. The most popular story is that of Caroline. Caroline was one of the previous owners that has passed on and seems to be having a hard time letting go. Recently Catfish Plantation got their liquor license, and an increase in activity was noted. This is believed to be due to the fact that Caroline was anti-alcohol. There are several other reports of possible spirits there, Will, a farmer who died in the house, as well as Elizabeth, who is reported to be seen in her wedding dress. Many psychics and others have reported even more possible spirits in the location but these are the ones I heard the most consistent stories about.

During an event we were holding at the location, a local paranormal team assisted with hosting the event. The events included a night of food and investigating for about twenty five people. The purpose of the events are to give people a small dose of being able to investigate the location alongside experienced investigators. The local team had a DVR system set up with cameras throughout the location. In one of the dining rooms, it was brought to my attention that there appeared to be something moving on the table on the DVR monitor. As I watched, it looked as if a sheet, or piece of paper, was being blown or lifting up off the table. It did it every few minutes. I walked into the dining room and looked at the table on the camera. The was absolutely nothing on the table. No paper. No napkins. Just a bare table. I called out on the walkie-talkie and they could still see it on the screen, but I could not see it looking directly at it. Confused, I asked one of the other investigators to come inside and stand where I was, while I went out to watch the screen myself. I could see it plain as day on the screen. Every few seconds it would move, almost in floating fashion. I could see the investigator standing next to it, and he, like I, was not seeing anything at all.

On one of the nights we were investigating, we were in a different dining room. Present in the room was myself, Buffy, Jimmy, the owner's daughter Shawn, and her husband David. During the time spent in this room, we heard several voices that seemed to be almost having conversation, yet no one was talking. As I was sitting there, I noticed an extreme drop in temperature, and started to feel something tugging at the back of my shirt near my neck. I reached back, and nothing was there. My neck was freezing cold and Jimmy ran over to take a reading with the digital thermometer. The area directly behind me was seven degrees cooler than the rest of the room. In order to keep my hands free, I wear a miniature flashlight one my ear. It resembles a blue tooth for cell phones. At one point after feeling the tug on my shirt, I began to feel something moving the flashlight attached to my ear. As I called out that something was touching my ear, Buffy was able to point the camera in my direction and zoom in. On the video, you can actually see my shirt being moved as if being tugged, and see the flashlight attached to my ear begin to lift up. It moves up slightly, then as if let go, flops back down and begins to swing off my ear. This was the first instance of being touched that I had experienced. I have been to many locations, but had never had anything like this happen before.

In yet another dining room, I was with the same group of people, and we were taunting one of the suspected spirits. Several things happened during this time. We had temperature drops, EMF hits, and probably the biggest of things, a chair moved. Shortly after the taunting stopped, we asked it to move one of the chairs. I heard a sliding sound next to me, and out of the corner of my eye, the chair between Shawn and I moved slightly. Jimmy, who was across the room, saw it too and immediately snapped his head up to look in our direction. As we discussed what we saw, and how we thought it was a trick of the light rather than the chair actually moving, it moved again, only this time it slid about a foot away. I looked directly at Shawn and asked her if she touched the chair, she confirmed that she didn't, and said that she tought I had moved it. The chair was a good three feet away from me, and probably another three away from Shawn, so there was no way either of us could have moved it. I was able to catch this on video, and the chair glides in a very smooth motion, with almost a supernatural look to it.

During another investigation, our medium was able to pick up on several things that we were able to confirm as accurate by some of the reports given at the restaurant. During part of the investigation in "Caroline's Room", our medium felt as though she had been touched on the elbow. So it would seem that this place has quite a bit of physical interaction. I have been there several times and seen movement of shadows in the hallway near the bathroom, and experienced hearing voices throughout the location while we were the only ones inside. Several times we also experienced what is said to be the most common activity there. No matter how many times you set up silverware in a specific formation on the table, within thirty minutes, the silverware will be moved. It will either be spread and facing different directions than what you left them in, or they will cross each other completely in the shape of an X. The first few times this happened I was thinking that it was possible someone could have just bumped the table causing them to move. Finding out that was not the case, we tried several other experiments. We placed the silverware and then tested out walking and jumping on certain areas of the floor to see if any loose boards might be bumping the table legs or something causing the knives and forks to move. Nothing we did, short of shaking the table itself by hand, caused the cutlery to move. As a last ditch effort, we set them up and walked out of the building leaving it completely empty. There was no one inside, and we sat out on the patio with everyone to make sure no one went inside. After about twenty minutes, we went back inside, and the silverware had moved on its own again.

There are plenty of other stories of things that happened at Catfish Plantation, but these are the most prominent ones that I experienced firsthand. If you ever have the chance to go there, the chances are, you will probably experience at least one thing there. I saved one of the main stories for you to find out on your own. If you are ever in the area, or decide to make the trip for the amazing food, try to find Shawn or David and ask them to tell you the story of Pete. Pete is a unique "spirit" that makes his presence known in several ways. If you happen to experience Pete's presence while you are there, it's guaranteed to be something you won't forget, and his story will creep you out while you enjoy your sweet potato fries with white chocolate sauce.

Two-Steppin' Into the Past

Another great Texas location is found in the Stockyards of Fort Worth. During one particular visit to Texas, another paranormal team that I had been acquainted with invited me, our team medium, and Buffy, to tag along with their team to do an investigation of Miss Molly's Hotel. This place still has the look and feel of early western days. Walking up to the building, I could almost picture being a cowboy rolling into town and heading for the saloon. It was a neat atmosphere. Miss Molly's was built in the early 1900s and has seen its share of action. Besides being a popular hotel, it was also a bordello. There are many stories surrounding the haunting of the location. Things from full bodied apparitions to noises and luminous vapors have been experienced there.

We met up with the associate team and settled on a plan to attack the location in the most effective manner. Our friend, Jimmy, was also present at this investigation and he and I ventured on our own for most of the night. There were a ton of methods being used for this as well as different variations of equipment. I took it upon myself to make the most of this investigation by trying to find an explanation for one of the most notorious apparitions reported there; the cowboy. People have reported seeing this shadowy figure in the shape of a man wearing a cowboy hat walking the halls between the rooms at Miss Molly's. I began to search out for what could be causing people to see this shadow, and to be honest, I found the cause by complete accident.

After all of the lights were turned out and everyone was settled, Jimmy and I walked into one of the bedrooms adjacent from the stairs to grab extra batteries. An EVP session was being held in the front room, but the audio for the night would prove to be useless. There is a bar downstairs directly below, and the sounds of the music being played carried all the way up into the hotel, so there was too much interference to get solid audio. As we began to walk out of the bedroom, I saw the shadow. It looked as if a six foot tall man wearing a cowboy hat darted right in front of me. It startled me, and I immediately told Jimmy to begin filming in that direction with hopes that it would happen again. As I walked closer to the staircase, it happened again, but this time on the opposite wall. It was clear and distinguishable. It had definite shape to it. I took a step back, and just as I did, the shadow appeared again. I took another step back, and it appeared to move the opposite direction. At this point, I had it figured out. I looked at the shape of the top of the staircase. My flashlight, attached to my ear, would shine against the railing, and cast the shadow of the top of the post along the wall. The peculiar shape of the post was causing the "cowboy hat". I called the members of the other team over and showed them what we had stumbled upon.

For most of the night, small things would happen here and there. We would get knocks and bangs when we asked for them, sounds of footsteps could be heard while everyone was sitting still, and a few investigators claimed to have a feeling of being touched and even having their hair pulled. There was something, however, that made this whole investigation worthwhile. Inside the room known as the "Railroader", which was a train themed room, we experienced something strange. Jimmy and I were standing just outside the door to the room. It was open and being held in place by a kickstand. As Jimmy and I started to talk, I heard what sounded like the door creaking. This was a heavy door, but the kickstand was holding it firmly and had no give to it at all. I turned to Jimmy and asked him if he had noticed whether or not the door had been doing this all night. He confirmed it had not, and in mid sentence, it made a noise as if it was about to slam shut. Jimmy and I became excited and started to head into the room.

As I walked into the room, I was met with a very cold chill and the feeling that I had stepped into the biggest spider web known to man. Every part of my body, especially my arms began to tingle. I had goose bumps on my arms and every hair was standing on end. It felt like a pocket of intense static electricity. I took out my Mel Meter which is an EMF detector that also measures temperature, and sat it on the floor in front of the door. I squatted down and put my hands out about four inches away from the door itself. I asked several times for whatever it was to push the door hard enough to come to my hands. This would have been near impossible since with the kickstand, we ourselves were not able to do it. Every few seconds the door would creak as if something was pushing it, and each time it would creak, the reading on the EMF detector would spike up by over four points. It did this for nearly an hour. It was curious how the timing of the EMF spike and the sound of the door attempting to move were in synch with each other. If the theory is correct, then we may have actually experienced an entity trying to manipulate a physical object, and in the process, the energy being exerted was causing the fluctuation on the meter.

This was the bigger of the experiences had at Miss Molly's that night, and while it wasn't something overly exciting, it was the first time I had seen a correlation like that between an object and the electromagnetic field. I did not get a chance to explore many of the other rooms since my focus was mainly on the "cowboy ghost", and the door incident. In talking to several of the other investigators, they each claimed to have some sort of unique experience happen to them while in the hotel.

If given the opportunity to ever go back, I would love to go on a night when there are no bands playing downstairs. I am not sure if that would mean having to come back on a particular day of the week, or a particular time of year, but I would be willing to bet given the history of this location, that the possibility of picking up something incredible on the audio recorder would be fairly high. I am always fascinated by these type of locations, and would love to see how they operated in their day, how people experienced it when it was in its prime. I can almost picture the bustling bordello with the saloon piano playing downstairs. The cowboys rolling through town, having a drink, playing card games, getting into fist fights, and maybe a gun duel or two, just the thought of it makes it worth it to me.

HILL HOUSE MANOR

When I first heard the name Hill House Manor, I immediately thought about places like Hell House, and House on the Hill, so naturally I was excited to get a unique opportunity. Our team medium had investigated the location before with a previous team that she was a part of, and our fellow investigator Jimmy was good friends with the owners of the house. I didn't know what excited me the most, the stories of the activity they had there, or the fact that I heard they served the best hotdogs in Gainesville, Texas. When we arrived at the location, I made good use of their hotdog cooker prior to investigating.

We met up with Linda, the owner, and had her tell us about the different things that have gone on there. We heard plenty of experiences, not just of her own, but of the paranormal teams that have come through there and had overnight investigations. The house itself has a curious history about it. It seemed to have unique hallways and strangely placed doors. Because of this, they believe that it may have been a speak easy, providing ample access to escape in the event of a raid.

Previous investigators have witnessed everything from the movement of objects, feelings of being touched, voices, and strange equipment readings on the EMF detectors. There have also been lots of photos with anomalies in them such as faces, and what appears to be a light in the shape of a young child. Jimmy himself had captured a photo while there with his team that seemed to be a face in the reflection of up an upstairs door. I always like to look at the photos and other collected evidence prior to investigating in hopes that during the night we either find a reason for the anomalies, or we experience the same things ourselves to validate the other experiences.

After taking the tour, the team medium and I began to set up along with Jimmy and one of his own team members. We started upstairs in a small bedroom. In this room, we had several different objects on a table and were trying to encourage some object manipulation. On a few occasions Jimmy and our medium both thought they heard a voice or the sounds of someone talking. In a mirror lining a closet door in this room, there was some tarnishing beneath the surface of the glass, and depending on the angle you stood, if you took a picture and used a flash on the camera, it would appear to have a face in the mirror. This was not the same spot, however, where Jimmy had previously caught the face in his photo. With not much going on in this room, we decided to leave an audio recorder running and move our group to an adjacent room,

This room appeared to be a kitchen type room. It had a checkered floor pattern, cabinets, and a sink. Our medium started using a set of dowsing rods in this room. The theory about the dowsing rods is that they will move when the magnetic field is manipulated. Some would say this is the same effect as an EMF detector, but the dowsing rods are subject to user manipulation. While it may not be on purpose, even the smallest of vibration in a steady hand can cause the rods to swing. During the session, the medium was able to get some pretty neat responses when asking the rods to cross, or to point to a specific person in the room. I personally have never put much stock into dowsing rods, but during her session, I monitored the EMF detector closely. It was interesting to see it register on the meter during the times the rods would move. During part of the session I was filming our medium with the video camera, and while the rods were moving, I noticed a strange light that seemed to move around her at the same time. It wasn't what I would typically call an orb or dust, and it moved in a very precise manner. I made note of this and we continued on. During the use of the dowsing rods, the medium told me that she could actually see the energy that appeared to be moving the rods. To the best of description I can compare it to, it was like the wavy distortion you see rising off the pavement on a hot day. Shortly after this session, I heard a strange noise come from the bathroom next to this room. I walked over, but never heard the sound again.

We made our way into what is called the "Window Room". This was a large room, with a table in the middle containing various objects, and completely surrounded by windows. We decided not to take many photos in this room due to the large amount of reflective surfaces that could cause reflections and false positives. We continued on with EVP sessions and attempts to generate responses and object manipulation. Several times, we heard noises just outside this room in another part of the house. The noises were faint and we couldn't determine the source, but we all agreed to head down to the basement and continue our investigation.

For me, this is when the night got interesting. Basements are creepy in general, and for some reason, most people fear basements and attics more than any other rooms in a house. As we set up, we split up and explored the area. I was in the process of setting up a full spectrum camera on a tripod aimed at the far room in the back. Jimmy was standing next to me, and Wes was directly behind us. As I was looking at the LCD screen on the back of the camera to see what I was framing up in the shot, I saw what looked like someone coming around the corner with a flashlight. I automatically assumed it was our medium and began taking pictures. I waited for her to come out of the room, but then I was caught off guard. I heard her speaking just off to my right. Jimmy and I looked at each other puzzled and I called out to her. She was near the staircase filming it, and nowhere near the room where I had the camera pointed. We called her over to us and explained that we just saw what looked like a person walking with a flashlight in the room directly in front of us. None of us were in that room, so we had no explanation. Jimmy's team member stated that he also saw it. As we were talking about it, the medium then saw the shadow move in the room and we all made our way there as quickly as we could. There was no one in there. We started setting up the equipment in there, and the medium once again began using the dowsing rods. We didn't see the shadow again, but during the session, the medium said she felt like something was touching her hair. I started filming her, and just as I turned the camera on her, I could see her hair being slightly raised, then fall back down. Jimmy also claimed that he felt something touch his arm.

We concluded our investigation after a couple more hours, and headed out. Jimmy has been back to Hill House Manor several times since we all went there. One of the last times he went, he was there alone and witnessed a full body apparition while trying to fall asleep. He has also caught EVPs, and other strange photos.

I would have to say that based on the things we saw and experienced at Hill House Manor, that there is definitely something going on there. I look forward to going back a few times and collecting more research of the location to see if I can find patterns in the activity. Most of the time you cannot get a full idea of all of the activity going on at a location in one visit, and in most cases, you will need to visit a location many times over several months to get proper documented results. With all of the people who also have experienced things here though, I would say you should head up there for a tour, or an overnight stay the next time you are in the area.

THE FREESTONE COUNTY MUSEUM

Back in March of 2010, I made one of my first trips to Texas. I was speaking at a conference south of Dallas. Among the many faces I met, I was approached by a woman and her fiancé about a location they were involved with. The woman was named Sandy, she was the current curator for the museum, and her counterpart was Andy. They had a photo of an old fire engine that was on the property of the museum they both worked at. There was what appeared to be a transparent man sitting in the driver seat of the fire engine, just behind the windshield. At first glance, my first thoughts were a play of light on a very old and dirty windshield, but there was something odd about the way it looked that piqued my interest. While telling me the story behind the photo, she also pointed out that there was an old 1800's jail on the property. At this point, I was completely sold, and I decided we would go down to the location and spend a night in the old jail before going home. Before leaving the convention, a couple of local investigators that had also taken an interest in the location, Jimmy Hanks and Shane Hobbs, agreed to investigate along with us. This is not the same Jimmy that has been out with us on other investigations. In fact, Jimmy and Shane were fairly new to organized team investigations and trying to establish their team, so we felt it would be a good learning experience for them.

We drove down to Fairfield, TX where the Freestone County Museum was located. The location was spread out over a few buildings besides the jail including old family cabins, an old bootleggers church, and the main museum building. Most of these had been moved to this location from another property. Being that this place had a lot of history behind it, we did not want to pre-dispose our medium to any advance information so Jimmy, Shane, and I took a tour with Sandy while the medium remained behind. Her job would be to walk the location and pick up on any feelings or possible readings she may get without hearing any of the stories. As we finished the tour, we met back up with her and the entire group congregated in the main building for the museum.

As with all new or inexperienced investigators, it's pretty common to see them get excited for every little noise made while conducting the investigation. The building had its share of creaks, bangs, pops, and other noises. There was a particular incident where the banging was extremely loud and continuous. Our medium was standing closest to the back door and she called the noise to our attention. It sounded vaguely like a horse and cart passing through. Sandy exclaimed "That's the sound of horses that investigators hear all the time here." Shane was the next closest to the door, and we all made our way over there. As soon as Shane opened the door, there were a few raccoons banging around going through the trashcan. They didn't scare off too fast at first, so it was very obvious that they rummage those trashcans fairly often which could explain why other investigators have heard it on their unattended audio and did not have a chance to check out the noise exactly when it happened.

The only other thing that happened in this area that was interesting was during a session with the ghost box. Again, I do not put a lot of faith into it, but I did find this a bit curious. Exhausting all techniques during our session in the main building, we decided to do a ghost box session to close it out. During the session we kept hearing the word "case". It said this several times. Shortly after the last time saying it, we heard something come from the front room. It sounded as if something had shook one of the cases containing family artifacts and relics. It was probably just coincidental, but I did make special note of it. It was as if something really was communicating and telling us that it was going to make a noise on one of the cases.

We moved from the main building and went into the old bootleggers church. This small old church had been used to bootleg whiskey during prohibition. It was still intact, yet sitting on blocks after being moved from another location to this property. During this point of the night, Jimmy had gone up and stood at the altar where a preacher would have given his sermons. Shortly after that we started seeing what looked like shadowy movement in one of the dark corners. Jimmy then reacted saying something had touched his ear. He described it as his ear and back of his neck turning cold, then the feeling of someone flipping the top of his ear down. Our photos in the church turned up no new particular evidence. Again, during a ghost box session, the word "thirteen" was spouted out a few times. Thinking that this had no real significance, I told Sandy and Andy that our medium has strange things involving the number thirteen show up in her life. In conversation, I mentioned that I have the number thirteen tattooed on my arm. Sandy and Andy both jumped up. They also had tattoos of the number thirteen. So this was a very strange thing to happen. The ghost box had randomly said the number thirteen several times, and then we found out that almost everyone in the room had some sort of connection with that number.

There are two sets of cabins in the area. One set of cabins provided no interesting results, but the second set of cabins had something happen while we were there. After being inside for a few minutes we caught a scent of what smelled like fresh bread baking. This side of the cabin used to be where food was prepared so it is possible that it was just a residual smell embedded in the wooden walls. At one point, I saw a dark shadow move outside of the door. Our medium saw a second dark shadow go in front of the window. As we made our way outside, Jimmy and I heard what sounded like footsteps running through the grass just behind the jail. As we got closer we heard a shrieking sound that startled us all. Then we spotted it. Just off to our right, and in between the cabin and the old fire engine were a pair of fighting opossums. We are fairly sure they were the cause for the shadows and the sounds of footsteps in the grass.

It was finally time to enter the building that had been used for a jail. Hearing about it I had it pictured in my head that the interior still looked like a jail, but after taking the initial tour, I was somewhat disappointed. It had been converted to a boarding house later on, so it beared no resemblance of a jail inside. From the outside it still had the look. It was a solid two story brick building. Inside the place had several original artifacts from the jail days like the mobile prisoner bathtub. It was a small bathtub on wheels that everyone incarcerated had to share.

After we got everything set up, we began doing a sweep and immediately we all heard footsteps upstairs. Trying to keep the group from getting too excited, I told them that we needed to stay downstairs and observe the noises before heading up. Nothing really happened on the first floor other than hearing the things going on upstairs so we finally made our way up.

Once we reached the top of the stairs, we broke off into separate rooms. Our medium immediately started getting readings and picking up on impressions. It wasn't until we sat for the last session that her impression was revealed to us. As we sat in a circle, Jimmy was almost asleep, and Shane was on the verge of passing out as well. The medium began to tell us that she was picking up on two men. One was a dark figure. She said the two men were involved in a scuffle that resulted in the death of the other. She even spoke of one of the men being hit in the head with something metal. This was the first time I realized that this particular medium may have genuine abilities. Her reading was dead on.

Earlier during the tour, Sandy had given me a newspaper article about a man who was killed in jail. She told us the story as she gave us the tour in this same very spot. The two men were arguing over a pair of shoes. One was a colored man, and the other a young Caucasian male. During the struggle the Caucasian man struck the other man over the head with a small piece of iron that had been broken off an old stove. He beat him with it repeatedly until he no longer moved. He then popped his head out the barred up window and yelled for them to come get the man he just killed. This was not just a local legend. This was a documented fact, and printed in the newspaper with all of the details. I was given a copy of the article to keep. I showed this to our medium after we got back from the investigation to show her just how accurate she had been. She also picked up on an injury to a sheriff, and although she got the injury area on his body correct and the incident correct, she was not able to pick up on exactly where it happened.

At this point, Jimmy and Shane called it a night and made a long drive back to Dallas. The medium and I decided we were going to sleep in the jail overnight to see if anything happened by morning. We slept in the downstairs area with sleeping bags on the floor. Shortly after laying down I heard what sounded like hard soled boots walking across the floor upstairs. What was even more interesting was it also has a metallic sound as well that kind of sounded like spurs. Several times we would hear talking. We heard several conversations that sounded like two or more people. There was no one else in the building besides us, and no one was out on the streets. It was after four a.m. and I have to admit, with everything going on, I was having some trouble getting to sleep. I laid there in a strange state of awareness. Almost as if I didn't want to take my attention away from the noises or let my guard down. At some point the medium and I both finally passed out from being up too many hours. We awoke the next morning and met up with Sandy and Andy.

We spent about half of the day exploring the town and a

couple of other historic locations before heading out. The town is rich in history and some parts of it seem untouched. While the stuff we found at the Freestone County Museum wasn't solid concrete, we did have a few experiences that would make me want to return for another investigation. Some of the things we saw and heard could easily be explained, but I still don't know what to think of the sounds we heard upstairs in the old jail. It was a great experiment for our medium's abilities however, and that was something I had wanted to see, so it made the whole trip worth it.

THE EXPERIENCE OF A LIFETIME

The last experience I am going to talk about in this book is the one that left the largest standing impression on me. It happened so fast, but I saw it with my own eyes, less than five feet in front of me, and I was not alone.

I had heard about this location many times. I had seen it on popular television shows, and I had heard all of the firsthand accounts from people all over the east coast that had visited it and experienced unexplainable things there. I could not wait to get the opportunity to experience it for myself. Deep down I felt, like many other locations, that it was overhyped and I would end up disappointed. I was wrong.

The location was Sloss Furnaces in Birmingham, Alabama. I was there throwing a paranormal event with about a hundred people in attendance. Prior to the event, I had watched a few of the television shows that had visited this location recently, and I had also done a bit of studying up on the history and stories behind the location. It was very important in this particular case that we separate the fiction of the location from the facts.

To get to the point, let me start by saying, the ghost referred to as "Slag" does not exist. The story of Slag, also known as James Wormwood, is a fictional story created for the annual Halloween function called the "Sloss Fright Furnace". Slag is a completely made up story. A popular television show did an episode shot at this location and during their interview process, they were misinformed of this fact and quoted the lore as actual history. Viewers of this show, took this information as fact and ran with it. After speaking with historians and Sloss Furnaces on site expert, we were told that the story was indeed false and created by the masterminds behind their Halloween funhouse.

With that said, I feel I can move on and tell you about the real haunting of this location. Yes. Sloss Furnaces is haunted. It is one of the rare occasions that you will hear me use that sentence.

What I, and three other witnesses saw there, has me convinced.

As I stated before, this was an event that we were throwing for the general public. It allowed people to come into the location and mingle with paranormal enthusiasts and television personalities from their favorite shows. During the event, we had the crowd broken up into smaller groups, and we would rotate them from one area to the next every hour. During one of the rotations, a lull between groups happened. An investigator, myself, Ashley Godwin of Ghost Hunters International, and her husband Ryan, were left waiting alone for the next group to arrive.

Ryan, despite what his wife does for a living, does not believe in the paranormal, or should I say, didn't believe in the paranormal. As we stood together making small chat, strange things began to happen. We had gone to an area that my investigator felt we were not supposed to be, and that something was lurking in the darkness. After doing a small walk, we noticed that the next group still had not arrived. The investigator thought it would be a good idea to get some footage of the area known as the "breezeway" while no one was around. The four of us stood on the breezeway on the end closest to the staging area of Sloss Furnaces. As we looked down the long stretch of semi covered railroad tracks in the pitch black dark, Ryan and I noticed a small green light. It looked similar to when someone runs a flashlight across an animal's eye in the dark. It was close to the ground, and it was very bright. We decided to walk down the tracks to try and get a closer look to see what was causing it. My first thought was that somehow some light was reflecting on a small piece of broken glass or something, but that was not the case.

As we made our way down the tracks, the green light disappeared. I mostly used my camera viewfinder while walking as I had no flashlight, so my only way to see was through the night vision on the camera. Being as dark as it was, my external IR lights were not strong enough to light the whole area, and my camera was having a hard time staying in focus. The further down the tracks we went, the worse time I had trying to keep it focused. At one point, I believed to see movement during the moments of being blurred. The only way to keep the camera in focus was to point it down at the tracks, and allow it to focus on the ground. It was extremely tough to see after pointing the camera at the ground due to the brightness of the LCD screen causing a temporary blindness.

We got about three quarters of the way down the tracks and

very close to where we saw the original green light. I pointed my camera down to regain focus one last time and as I looked up and away to my right, I saw it. Less than about five feet away was only what I can refer to as an apparition. I saw a definite outline of shoulders, a torso, arms, and hands. Just as I saw it, I screamed "Oh, shit!", in the most professional manner possible, and just at that moment, the rest of the group saw it as well. My investigator and Ashley both screamed, and Ryan was too terrified to get an audible word to come out of his mouth. It shot at us in a fast swooping motion, almost reaching our face, then shot off immediately to our right and was gone. We were completely shaken at the core from this incident. There was no doubt about what we had seen and the fact that we all saw it.

I had never seen anything like this before. I remembered that my camera was running as I was walking, so all I could do was pray that I had caught this on camera. As I mentioned before, keeping the camera in focus was next to impossible, but I did manage to capture enough to validate our experience. The video looks nothing like what we saw with our own eyes. It was so out of focus, that the bright light it was illuminating make it come off as a large ball of light that looked as bright as a sun. What the video did show, however, was that while I had the camera pointed down the breezeway, there was nothing there, then in a single frame forward, there was a tiny flicker of light. It doubled in brightness in the next frame, then in a rapid but very smooth movement it shot at us with supernatural speed.

For the rest of the night, Ryan, who did not believe in the paranormal at all, was now convinced, and he was terrified. We could see it in his face. All he wanted to do was go home. It was hard mentally for myself to walk back down to the area just after it happened in fear of it still being right there waiting. It felt as if it had used the green light to bait us, or lure us in, and then in a single fleeting moment, it had jump at us to try and scare us. Had I not known better, I would have sworn it was someone playing a trick on us, using a projector or some other sort of device, but I knew there was no one else involved. It literally looked like a special effect you would see in a movie, and I only wish that the camera had caught it the same way that we had seen it.

We made a return trip to Sloss Furnaces about six months later, and we had the same people with us to try and create the same situation in hopes to see this anomaly again. The previous incident happened shortly after a train had passed by, along with other atmospheric ingredients, so we waited until the time was right, or at least similar to when it happened the first trip. We did not see it this time around. We may never see it again. It was one of those once in a lifetime things you hope to see, and from that point on, almost every location that I have visited has been a bit of a disappointment because of the experience at Sloss setting the bar so high. If you ever get an opportunity to visit Sloss Furnaces, whether it's just to walk around during the daytime, or if you get the chance to attend an event or investigation, I strongly suggest that you do so. This location made it to the top of my all time list for things that I have seen that I could not explain.

CHOOSE YOUR WEAPONS

As an investigator in an ever changing field of technology, many pieces of new equipment have become available. In the beginning there were very few reliable pieces of equipment and most investigators were limited to 35mm cameras, audio recorders, and electromagnetic field detectors. Most serious investigators found unconventional items here and there to assist with getting results, but there has never been a set rule on exactly which equipment is acceptable during investigations.

We are now living in a digital age. A lot of newer

technology becomes obsolete the minute it is removed from its packaging. Video cameras have gone from tape based to hard drive or memory card storage. Audio recorders have gone from cassette tapes, micro cassette tapes, and have progressed to superior studio quality digital recorders. In the mix of this growth of technology, a few ambitious people have found ways to improve upon or generate brand new equipment to benefit research.

One of the first questions I always get asked is about the equipment one should own when starting up their team. I always recommend the following minimums; a digital camera with a decent lens and highest megapixel count affordable, a digital audio recorder for holding EVP sessions, a video camera equipped with infrared night vision, a digital thermometer or newer technology such as the MEL-METER which registers electromagnetic field and temperature simultaneously, and most important of all, a level of common sense.

The most common mistake made by most investigators is using equipment before they properly understand its function and use. This mistake was made most apparent by the introduction to a new piece of equipment to the field several years ago called the K2 meter. Unlike previous EMF detectors, this particular device use a broadband pass sensor instead of the traditional hall effect sensor found in early models. The first generation K2 meter had a button that powered the device using a momentary switch, meaning the button had to be held down to establish the connection for the power to circulate through the device. This resulted in false reads as someone's thumb began to tire or the connection was not solid. It would cause the indicator lights on the top of the device to flash as if getting a reading. The only way to avoid this was to wedge a coin or other object into the switch to get a constant reading. Later versions corrected this with a push button that clicks into place and must be pressed again to turn the device off.

This was just a small portion of the problem posed by the K2 meter, however. The single biggest flaw is that it is also influenced by radio frequency. At any particular time, if you got a reading, there was nothing to distinguish whether it was an electromagnetic field or a radio frequency hit. So many other devices would cause interference on the K2 meter, particularly walkie talkie signals or nearby cell phones. I found a easy way to make this tool a little more useful, but to be honest a K2 meter is at the bottom of my priority list for "must own" equipment. They do seem to be popular though, as more and more teams now have them. My suggestion is to do exactly what I did. I found a small portable radio frequency detector about the size of a pack of gum and I attached it to my K2 meter. This way if we got a reading and the RF detector beeped, we knew it was a radio frequency and not an electromagnetic field. If it did not go off when the K2 lit up, then you have a legitimate electromagnetic field hit.

For other new advances, I am a huge fan of full spectrum technology. For years, we have all used night vision cameras which shoot in the infrared spectrum. These cameras have been used for two reasons; most people investigate in the dark because night time is quieter and by dimming your sight, your other senses become heightened, and because the camera shoots in a spectrum that is not visible to the naked eye.

Full spectrum has opened up a new door that wasn't

previously available. It includes the ultra-violet spectrum. Most of the time you can see the changes in the UV spectrum with the use of a black light, but most video cameras are built with a filter that blocks this unwanted spectrum out. Full spectrum cameras capture visible, infrared, and ultra-violet, thus increasing your chances of possibly seeing something that you would have not been seen with your own eyes.

Another piece of equipment making its rounds is the "Ghost Box" or "Shack Hack". This is a device that is believed to allow two way communication with any spirits or ghosts looking to talk. It creates a white noise as it sweeps through the channels and at times, you may get responses to questions you ask. It got the name "Shack Hack" because it started from a very popular Radio Shack AM/FM radio that you would "hack" into and allow it to be converted. The only thing that the hack consisted of is removing the MUTE pin from the circuit. The mute pin is common in most digital tuning radios. It basically silences all the noise between channels so that you don't have to hear annoying distortion when changing stations. It is also how the scanner knows to stop on a station. It will scan over the muted silence and find the stronger station before stopping. Who knew that all this time, the only thing keeping us from being able to talk to the dead was a single pin?

Although I do make light of the situation, I have seen results that seem to be more than coincidence. Most of the time I do believe that the answers most people believe they hear, is caused by the same thing that causes people to see shapes of animals in clouds, and faces in pictures. I can honestly say that ninety-nine percent of it turns out to be audio matrixing. Most people are asking questions that they already know the answer to so they are priming themselves to listed to the gibberish for words that sound similar to the answer they are waiting for. While this is not true in all cases, I feel that most of it can indeed be explained by this.

The Shack Hack is a budgeted version of a much larger device called the Frank's Box. The Frank's Box was built by Frank

Sumption and is a little different than just clipping a pin on a circuit board. Only a few people in the world own one of these devices and even less of them can actually use them correctly. I have seen a few of them in person and still draw the conclusion that the results are about as accurate or the same percentage as the Shack Hack.

So with all of the black light UV cameras, strobe lights, and other devices, all we need to get a great party started is a green laser. People have started using laser grids more and more frequently with mixed results. The purpose is to cast a grid down a hallway or along a wall, and anything passing through would cause a distortion or break in the grid. This is great for capturing shadow figures or full body apparitions. Most people use a small laser pointer on a mini tripod. I highly recommend that if you decide to use a laser grid that you purchase the large professional DJ lasers. The small pen lasers run off of batteries and as the batteries start to die, it will cause false positives as the lights begin to twinkle out. Another reason is because the pens are not meant to be used for extended periods of time. They have no built in resource for cooling the laser after running for more than a few minutes. This will cause the internal mechanisms to heat up and not function properly, and if left on for too long, the laser can cause damage to the glass lens which will also cause false positives and distortions in your grid.

The professional DJ laser has its own cooling fan and is made for long periods of use. It also has different settings so that you can make adjustments to your grid. After using the laser on several investigations I have found that they can be useful for setting "trap areas" and leaving a camera on them for the whole night. Use it in conjunction with other tools. One of my last setups had the laser grid, motion detectors, and a geophone (used for detecting vibrations such as footsteps). The combination of all of that equipment can really backup some of your experiences if all of them go off at the same time. I don't recommend that a novice investigator attempt to obtain all of this equipment as most of it will not be useful unless you are creative.

The last piece of equipment I am going to touch base on is the DVR system and why I have chosen to never use them. DVR camera systems have been the largest source of false positives picked up during investigations. They take the most preparation time from set up to break down than any other piece of equipment. You are also very limited to where your cameras can be placed depending on how much cable length you have to run them.

DVR cameras are typically low resolution and do not capture sound. While some of the newer systems have these features, it still does not fix the issue of portability. With the introduction of hard drive based cameras and cameras that run off of memory cards that shoot in high definition, I believe the DVR system to be obsolete. I would rather spend the same amount, or less depending on the brands, on decent cameras that record superior video and audio. They can be placed on mini tripods and run on battery power, meaning you are not limited to where you can place them. The audio and picture quality will be higher than that of any DVR system camera, so in my opinion, this is really a no-brainer. Besides, a not having a DVR system will free up an extra investigator from being stuck in front of a screen showing four or more camera angles all at once, only to have to watch it all again later. Besides, trying to watch four cameras at once can cause them to miss important things as it is hard to focus on just one area.

If you recall the earlier chapter for Mermaid Manor, the DVR proved to just be more trouble than it was worth and to an inexperienced investigator, the video captured on it would have ended up on the internet as "Proof of Ghosts". It is just better to eliminate any chances of false positives and go with individual cameras.

While there are tons of new equipment out there, I chose to talk about these a little because they seem to be the most popular. They all have their pros and cons, but really it's up to you. Most of the equipment being used today is unconventional because it was not designed for paranormal investigating. Luckily, we have all been smart enough to find ways to use it to help out, but we are using a lot of devices for purposes other than what they were intended for. The good news is, a lot of very innovative people have started putting ideas together and changing that for the field. Equipment is now being designed specifically with the paranormal in mind. I do not think we will have the answers to the paranormal in my lifetime, but I do hope all of the work we are doing now establishes the ground work for people to build on and make even more advances in the future.

Made in the USA
Charleston, SC
18 February 2013

Praise for Beneath Bethlehem Skies

"*Beneath Bethlehem Skies* is an original presentation of the encouragement so many of us need when we enter the Advent season each year: that we have eternal hope in the promise of Christ. Artfully bringing together Scripture, materials from contemporary and classical Christian saints, and his own compelling narrative, Brandon Anthony Shuman reminds us that Advent is not just a season; it is a miracle through which the living God comes to dwell with his people. I would encourage all who are weary, all who are strong, and all who desire to grow in their walk with the Lord to experience his transformative composition this Advent season."

Michael Lindsay, Ph. D.
President, Gordon College

"It seems to me that there is a deep yearning within the body to connect with and embrace the profound traditions passed down by the saints who have gone before us. *Beneath Bethlehem Skies* helps us make this connection and deepen our communion with our Lord and his church during this beautiful season. Brandon's writing paired with Rachel Long's skillful use of the ancient medium of watercolor, welcomes both young and old into the necessary tension of the already and not yet of Advent. Alluring light and symbolism rouse the imagination, remembrance and longing. Her creations are a visual feast for pilgrim believers to relish year after year and be filled with the hope of Christmas while we wait."

Reagan Hughes Harper
Miss Texas, 1997

"Framed by well chosen scripture verses, Christmas carols, and incisive quotes from Christian thinkers past and present, Brandon Anthony Shuman's beautifully written advent devotionals join together philosophical, theological, and aesthetic insight with a strong historical sense of the ancient world. They will still your heart and open your eyes and ears to the wonder and joy of Christmas."

Louis Markos, Ph. D.
Professor in English and Scholar in Residence, Houston Baptist University
Author of *From Achilles to Christ* and *On the Shoulders of Hobbits.*

"Every Advent for the last decade my friend Brandon has read a piece of original Christmas writing for our church. Every year his words have blessed our body and caused us to reflect more deeply upon what is, in reality, an unfathomable reality . . . that our Creator came to earth and took on the form of a creature. After many seasons of sharing his insightful reflections with our church family, Brandon is finally sharing them with the wider world."

Tim Dunn
CEO of CrownQuest Operating
Author of *Yellow Balloons*

"Far more than candles and calendars, Advent is about a Christ who has, will, and is come. *Beneath Bethlehem Skies* is a creative, substantive resource that will help every heart to prepare him room. Read. Reflect. Renew. Rejoice."

Todd D. Still, Ph. D.
Charles J. and Eleanor McLerran DeLancey Dean &
William M. Hinson Professor of Christian Scriptures
Baylor University, Truett Seminary

"*Beneath Bethlehem Skies* is a beautiful and creative work from the heart. The passages from Scripture, excerpts from other writers, watercolors, and hymns all complement the words Brandon so eloquently puts on paper as he takes us through the season of Advent. As followers of Christ, we celebrate Christmas every day, but this intentional 26-day journey stirs my heart and mind toward the awe and wonder of the first Christmas. Brandon truly captures the tension we often feel as we live in a broken world full of pain yet also look to the hope we have for the future if we know Christ."

Rachel Shelton
Former Women's Director at T bar M camps
Former Director of Community and Director in Young Adults at Watermark Community
Church

"This book of Advent devotionals is excellent. Anyone can profit from Brandon's work of spiritual writings."

David K. Naugle, Ph. D.
Professor of Philosophy, Distinguished University Professor at Dallas Baptist University
Author of *Worldview: The History of a Concept* and *Reordered Loves, Reordered Lives:
Learning the Deep Meaning of Happiness*

"Hope, despair, brokenness, survival and redemption . . . Rich in both historical and biblical references, Brandon Anthony Shuman in *Beneath Bethlehem Skies* eloquently addresses these complex questions by pointing to the significance of that moment when God became man on Christmas in Bethlehem. The redemptive-historical framework Shuman deploys provides readers a true thoughtful path for hope in Jesus in the midst of moaning among the creatures between the paradoxical realities of 'already' but 'not-yet' of the Kingdom of God. A brilliant book for every Christian and those who are searching for true hope!"

Bob Fu, Ph. D.
Founder and President of ChinaAid
Author of *God's Double Agent*

"Inviting, compelling, and Christ-honoring describes Brandon Anthony Shuman's reflections of the Incarnate Son of God as experienced in Bethlehem Skies. Participants are engaged in a multi-sensory experience that stirs the affections toward thankfulness for God's great love and redemption as seen in the Greatest Story Ever Known. You will not be the same after experiencing these daily Advent selections."

Amy Avampato
Head Administrator of the Grammar School at Midland Classical Academy

"Like an Amazon package placed at your doorstep on Christmas Eve, Brandon Anthony Shuman delivers an Advent gift that is at once welcome and unexpected. He offers the reader a depth of Christmas insight that is full of color, character, and textures while making the fullness of it all accessible to young and old. *Beneath Bethlehem Skies* will become a treasured tradition for those who seek the true reality and gracious effect of Immanuel, God with us."

Randy Sims
Executive Pastor at Midland Bible Church
Founder Emeritus of Worldview Academy

"I have had the privilege of knowing Brandon Shuman since the summer of 1995. He had just completed his freshman year in high school, and I had just become his Student Minister. I was able to watch him grow up, mature, finish high school, go through college, marry a wonderful girl, and become a great husband and father. I say all of that to say this, I probably know Brandon about as well as anyone outside of his immediate family. His love for God is genuine, his heart is pure, his theology is solid, his priorities are in order, and his desire in life is to please God. All of that is reflected in this book, *Beneath Bethlehem Skies*. I was greatly blessed by the devotions I read, and I know that you will be, too. I highly commend this book to you."

Jon Redmond, Ph. D.
Associate Pastor
First Baptist Church in Pasadena, Texas

"In *Beneath Bethlehem Skies*, my friend, Brandon Shuman has done a rare thing. In brief but beautifully crafted essays, he has captured the heart and depth of the Christmas story. He has also successfully brought a new dimension to the traditional Christmas devotional with great insight and thought-provoking truth that will challenge the reader to stop and ponder and prayerfully consider anew the birth of Christ. These essays will be read year after year as they help uncover the amazing entrance of God into His creation. Well done, Brandon!"

Mark Rae
Executive Director of Grace Center for Spiritual Development
Grace School of Theology

"Beneath Bethlehem Skies is a feast for the senses and a compelling guide to reflect on the miracle of God becoming man. Shuman lays a banquet of Scripture and song, sparkling literary and historical quotes, and inspiring reflections that lead us to consider the human condition and how God both inhabits and transforms that reality through redemption and grace. Highly recommended for families, churches, and small groups as they reflect on Jesus as the incarnation of the Word of God."

Nick Ellis, Ph. D.
CEO of GDiGlobal

BENEATH BETHLEHEM SKIES

26 ADVENT MEDITATIONS UPON THE
MIRACLE AND MEANING OF
JESUS'S BIRTH

BRANDON ANTHONY SHUMAN

Published by Thousand Grain Press.
www.thougsandgrainpress.com

www.brandonanthonyshuman.com

Printed in the United States of America

Unless otherwise indicated, Scripture taken from the New King James Version®. Copyright © 1982 by Thomas Nelson. Used by permission. All rights reserved.

Edited by Nancy Haight
Cover Design and Interior Layout: Ryan Scheife of Mayfly Design

Library of Congress Cataloging-in-Publication Data
Shuman, Brandon Anthony
Beneath Bethlehem Skies: 26 Advent meditations upon the miracle and meaning of Jesus's birth / Brandon Anthony Shuman

Includes watercolor images

ISBN 978-1-7354403-0-9 (hardcover)
ISBN 978-1-7354403-1-6 (paperback)
ISBN 978-1-7354403-2-3 (ebook)

Religious. 2. Christmas. 3. Devotional. 4. Spirituality. 5. Advent.

For more information about the book or author, visit www.brandonanthonyshuman.com and follow our Facebook fan page "Bethlehem Skies."

To all those who have helped me to see Jesus and His Kingdom amidst the raging affairs of Babel: John Litton, Dr. Jon Redmond, Dr. David Naugle, Mark Kaufmann, A.J. Perea, Ron Miller, Dennis and Marilyn Stafford, Tim Dunn, Chris Craig, Mark McLane, Vince Loftis, and so many more.

To my wife, Laura, who is a living sacrament of God's grace.

To my parents, Rick and Toni Shuman,
who introduced me to Jesus at an early age.

And to my three children—Rowan, Eli, and beautiful Selah—for whom
I now bear the happy burden of acquainting with their Savior.

"The great majority of people will go on observing forms that cannot be explained; they will keep Christmas Day with Christmas gifts and Christmas benedictions; they will continue to do it, and someday suddenly wake up and discover why."

– G.K. Chesterton

Contents

Preface

"The celebration of Advent is possible only to those who are troubled in soul, who know themselves to be poor and imperfect, and who look forward to something greater to come. For these it is enough to wait in humble fear until the Holy One himself comes down to us, God in the child in the manger. God comes."

—Dietrich Bonhoeffer (1906–1945),
sermon from December 2, 1928

The first composition of *Beneath Bethlehem Skies* was written over ten years ago. As the calendar turned to December that year, my heart was mired in dissonance. Palpable, but inarticulate disappointments were shading my life and dimming my perspective. Externally, everything was fine. I was happily married and enthusiastic about my small part in God's Kingdom. But in my soul, there was a heaviness, and I felt a weariness of breath I could not name. Deep within there was a persistent ache and a longing for things to be set right.

At that time in my life, I regularly journaled my prayers, but I have always been more of a reader than a writer. For some reason one evening, as I thought about Christmas, I felt compelled to put into words the tensions wrestling about within me. On one side were the present and real frustrations I was experiencing. On the other were the even more real divine promises taking hold of me. Writing those words was something of an epiphany for my faith. For faith is, after all, living with joy amidst the tension between present pain and future hope. It was from within this same tension—on a scale paradoxically more cosmic and more personal—that God entered our world on a night long ago in Bethlehem.

I have revisited the manger in Bethlehem many times since that Christmas, often with a weary soul. But after each encounter, my faith was enlarged. As I began to share these expressions with others, I found that Christ often met them with similar encouragement and blessings. It is in this hope that I now share them with you.

It is my prayer that this book, with its words and images, along with the accompanying album, with its thoughts and music, will be an epiphany of faith for you this Christmas. Through them, may God remind you of the hope you have in Him, may Christ fill your life with His presence and restore your mind to peace, may the Father pour out His joy upon you, and may the Spirit open your heart to His love.

This is not just me sharing my thoughts on Advent. Included in these writings are astonishing expressions from faithful Christians throughout all ages who beautifully and timelessly captured the miracle of the Word becoming flesh.

Beneath Bethlehem Skies is not a Bible study or a neatly packaged devotional designed to give you a quick word to get you through the day. It is a series of reflective compositions saturated with truths from Holy Scripture. It is fraught with frailty and doubt even as it is filled with the power and promise of God's love. Its aims are to humble us to the meaning of the miracle of Advent and to awaken our heavy eyes to the face of Jesus.

—Brandon Anthony Shuman, Midland Texas, August 2020

December 1

Scriptural Prologue: The Prophecies

Genesis 3:15

"And I will put enmity
Between you and the woman,
And between your seed and her Seed;
He shall bruise your head,
And you shall bruise His heel."

Isaiah 9:1–7

Nevertheless the gloom will not be upon her who is distressed,
As when at first He lightly esteemed
The land of Zebulun and the land of Naphtali,
And afterward more heavily oppressed her,
By the way of the sea, beyond the Jordan,
In Galilee of the Gentiles.

The people who walked in darkness
Have seen a great light;
Those who dwelt in the land of the shadow of death,
Upon them a light has shined.

You have multiplied the nation
And increased its joy;
They rejoice before You
According to the joy of harvest,
As men rejoice when they divide the spoil.

For You have broken the yoke of his burden
And the staff of his shoulder,
The rod of his oppressor,
As in the day of Midian.
For every warrior's sandal from the noisy battle,
And garments rolled in blood,
Will be used for burning and fuel of fire.

For unto us a Child is born,
Unto us a Son is given;
And the government will be upon His shoulder.
And His name will be called
Wonderful, Counselor, Mighty God,
Everlasting Father, Prince of Peace.

Of the increase of His government and peace
There will be no end,
Upon the throne of David and over His kingdom,
To order it and establish it with judgment and justice
From that time forward, even forever.
The zeal of the Lord of hosts will perform this.

Isaiah 11:1–12

There shall come forth a Rod from the stem of Jesse,
And a Branch shall grow out of his roots.
The Spirit of the Lord shall rest upon Him,
The Spirit of wisdom and understanding,
The Spirit of counsel and might,

The Spirit of knowledge and of the fear of the Lord.
His delight is in the fear of the Lord,
And He shall not judge by the sight of His eyes,
Nor decide by the hearing of His ears;
But with righteousness He shall judge the poor,
And decide with equity for the meek of the earth;
He shall strike the earth with the rod of His mouth,
And with the breath of His lips He shall slay the wicked.
Righteousness shall be the belt of His loins,
And faithfulness the belt of His waist.

"The wolf also shall dwell with the lamb,
The leopard shall lie down with the young goat,
The calf and the young lion and the fatling together;
And a little child shall lead them.
The cow and the bear shall graze;
Their young ones shall lie down together;
And the lion shall eat straw like the ox.
The nursing child shall play by the cobra's hole,
And the weaned child shall put his hand in the viper's den.
They shall not hurt nor destroy in all My holy mountain,
For the earth shall be full of the knowledge of the Lord
As the waters cover the sea.

And in that day there shall be a Root of Jesse,
Who shall stand as a banner to the people;
For the Gentiles shall seek Him,
And His resting place shall be glorious."

It shall come to pass in that day
That the Lord shall set His hand again the second time
To recover the remnant of His people who are left,
From Assyria and Egypt,
From Pathros and Cush,
From Elam and Shinar,

From Hamath and the islands of the sea.

He will set up a banner for the nations,
And will assemble the outcasts of Israel,
And gather together the dispersed of Judah
From the four corners of the earth.

Micah 5:2–5

But you, Bethlehem Ephrathah,
Though you are little among the thousands of Judah,
Yet out of you shall come forth to Me
The One to be Ruler in Israel,
Whose goings forth are from of old,
From everlasting.

Therefore He shall give them up,
Until the time that she who is in labor has given birth;
Then the remnant of His brethren
Shall return to the children of Israel.

And He shall stand and feed His flock
In the strength of the LORD,
In the majesty of the name of the LORD His God;
And they shall abide,
For now He shall be great
To the ends of the earth;
And this One shall be peace.

December 2

The Hope of Christmas

"The Christmas message is that there is hope for a ruined humanity—hope of pardon, hope of peace with God, hope of glory—because at the Father's will Jesus became poor, and was born in a stable so that thirty years later He might hang on a cross. It is the most wonderful message the world has ever heard, or will hear."

—J.I. Packer (1926–Present) *Knowing God*

I will lift up my eyes to the hills
From whence comes my help?

My help come from the LORD,
Who made heaven and earth.

—Psalm 121:1-2

The Hope of Christmas

*H*ope.

We live in a broken world where stock markets crash, loved ones suffer, friends and family grow apart, and everything from international politics to stop lights are beyond our control. It doesn't seem to matter whether it's Murphy's law or the second law of thermodynamics, everything seems to break down. Each day we witness a thousand hurts and injustices crying out to be fixed, but what can we do? This brokenness extends even to ourselves as we fail to live up to all that we ought to be. We are all clocks that keep imperfect time.

This is not meant to be overly pessimistic, because there is much that is good and beautiful in the world, but we can all confess, to at least some degree, there are times when we have our doubts things will ever truly be right.

We all want peace and happiness, and we want it so badly that we are willing to place our hope in people, governments, educations, careers, policies, medicines, technologies, financial institutions, and religions, which are all bound to fail. But each time we are left disappointed, we still have the gumption to pick ourselves up and find something new to enchant us and to believe in. We willingly ignore all the warnings, suggesting we are only setting ourselves up for more heartache because we desperately want there to be something more. We would rather believe in a false hope, pretending it to be real, than go on without any hope at all. Hope is necessary for survival when we live in a world such as this. In a world such as this, often, hope is all we have.

Two thousand years ago, there was a small, insignificant nation occupied by a foreign power, with customs and laws contrary to its own. This nation had struggled for its sovereignty from its very inception and had somehow survived countless invasions, political realignments, and even exile. This nation was told by God that they were His chosen people, but all the evidence pointed to the contrary. What importance could God possibly have for a tiny farming nation that had been suppressed by four different civilizations far mightier than itself during the last four hundred years? Surely, if God wanted to make anything of them, He would have done so long before now. If there ever was a time when they were important in His sight, that time had passed. Despite any promises given in some lost age, it was apparent to everyone they were a nation destined to be forgotten by God and enslaved by others. As the reality of these sentiments descended upon the hearts of some lowly shepherds, a bursting light scattered the night, and they were told the very best news man had ever heard.

Christmas is important because it reminds us of the true reason to hope in the midst of a thousand evidences to despair. Christmas assures us God has not abandoned us to the horror of our own devices in a cold and empty universe. By entering our fallen world, assuming a body of corruption, enduring the afflictions of hunger and disease, feeling the pains of both body and soul, facing the scorns and abuse of men, Christ affirms not only His love for a fallen race, but also the potential for goodness and beauty rightly belonging to creatures once described as "the image of God."

The world did not become perfect when God entered our cosmos, nor did it become so when He returned to heaven. But let us not think He has come in vain. He will complete the work He has begun. The story of Christmas tells us He has come once. The hope of Christmas promises us He will come again, and when He does, all other hopes will be fulfilled. ●

Personal Reflections

- What false hopes most appeal to your heart?
  - How does Advent give you hope?

Hymn of Response

Good Christian Men Rejoice

Good Christian men rejoice
With heart and soul and voice!
Give ye heed to what we say
News! News!
Jesus Christ is born today!
Ox and ass before Him bow
And He is in the manger now
Christ is born today!
Christ is born today!

Good Christian men, rejoice
With heart and soul and voice
Now ye hear of endless bliss
Joy! Joy!
Jesus Christ was born for this
He hath ope'd the heav'nly door
And man is blessed evermore
Christ was born for this
Christ was born for this

Good Christian men, rejoice
With heart and soul and voice
Now ye need not fear the grave:
Peace! Peace!
Jesus Christ was born to save
Calls you one and calls you all
To gain His everlasting hall
Christ was born to save
Christ was born to save

—Heinrich Suso (14th Century)

December 3

Christmas without Christmas

"Who can add to Christmas? The perfect motive is that God so loved the world. The perfect gift is that He gave His only Son. The only requirement is to believe in Him. The reward of faith is that you shall have everlasting life."

—Corrie Ten Boom (1892–1983) (attributed)

"Who among us will celebrate Christmas correctly? Whoever finally lays down all power, all honor, all reputation, all vanity, all arrogance, all individualism beside the manger; whoever remains lowly and lets God alone be high; whoever looks at the child in the manger and sees the glory of God precisely in his lowliness."

—Dietrich Bonhoeffer (1906–1945)
sermon from December 17, 1933

Therefore we must give the more earnest heed to the things we have heard, lest we drift away.

—Hebrews 2:1

Christmas without Christmas

Nothing is so invisible as that which is omnipresent. God moves in plain sight, but our faithless eyes do not see. The loving voice of God strongly summons all near, but our ears are deaf to Heaven. The powerful hands of God daily carry us in His arms, but our proud souls are too swollen and callous to feel His gentle strength. God's love is now sustaining every moment, but the self-absorbed are oblivious to grace. To the proud, nothing is as invisible as God.

And so it is with Christmas, that holiday celebrating the crossroads of history—that moment when God first came near. It has maintained the same spot on the calendar for centuries. Its anticipation is unrivaled, building up for weeks until at last the morning arrives. It even has its own brand of music dedicated to get us into its holiday spirit. And lest we forget, before our Thanksgiving turkeys are cooked, we are bombarded with advertisements of all shapes and sizes reminding us of its hastening approach. But unless we are diligent, Christmas comes and goes unnoticed, un-cheered, and without care.

Do not miss Christmas this Christmas, for Christmas easily passes by.

Every year, another December goes busily by with another Christmas wasted and ignored. Christmas is the most glorious day of all, yet no other day is more neglected or forgotten. We are sooner to groan a dentist appointment or endure an oil change than to celebrate Christmas joy.

Our tendency to miss Christmas is perhaps the single likeness linking our Santa-cized holiday with that first holy night. How few then, as now, took notice of the Baby born in a Bethlehem stable? The star shone for all to see, but only the Magi lifted their gaze to perceive its light. Prophecies foretold His coming, but who had awareness to welcome Him? From Caesar in Rome counting his empire, to the inn keeper of Bethlehem counting his profits, to we who are making our lists and checking them twice—all fail to receive God in our midst.

In our haste, we hurry. In our neglect, we forget. In our angst, we fritter ourselves away one worry at a time. We are consumed by the all-consuming, pop holiday. After the decorating, the parties, the shopping, the baking, the wrapping, and the traveling are done, the only thing left untended is our weary hearts. Christmas at last arrives; its dawn finds that we have not prepared ourselves for its advent. Surrounded by glittering tinsel and wrapping, our souls thin and fade. As the presents are unwrapped, *we* are no longer present, for there is no longer an *"us"* to receive them. Thus, we have become too busy, too scattered, and too rushed to enjoy Christmas's greatest gifts.

We have heard every note but not the melody. We have seen every light but are not warmed by their glow. In the unending parade of December, we have marched every step but missed Christmas's meaning. Sadly, amidst it all, we have somehow become souls without Christmas.

How can we discover its magic? Where must we pilgrim to uncover its message? Where is its meaning revealed?

Like a child first aware that she is lost, these are the natural questions we raise. But Christmas is not a matter of being found, for it is omnipresent and was never lost. Rather, it is we who are disoriented and in need of being found. We do not find Christmas, for Christmas is the story of God finding us. In hearing the Christmas Gospel, we discover that it is we who have been found. Christmas gives us back to ourselves. In giving us Himself, God has reclaimed us.

Christmas gives us both God and ourselves. Christmas enables us to both know God and to be known by God. Christmas is the gift of God's love for us. It establishes us in Heaven and upon the earth. This is the angels' praise of God's reconciliation.

Through Advent, God entered our world, touched our beings and lit our souls ablaze with life. The force of Advent is awesome and powerful, stronger than sorrow, stronger than death, more dynamic than life. But Advent, like the child for whom it is celebrated, speaks in faithful whispers year after year, December after December, and every day in between.

Though Bethlehem's star has dimmed, the True Light still shines. Immanuel's eternal presence is still among us. Hope abounds. Are we so busy planning "Christmas" that we do not know it has arrived? Can we not hear the songs of angels? God's love is transforming every situation. Do we have the eyes to see? Do we not have hands to serve and hearts to love? Every moment is pregnant with the potential of Christmas. May we all have the faith, hope, and love to engage with the presence of God in the stables of life. As we set up the tree, string out the lights, and exchange gifts with those we love, may Heaven's light find us, and may we share its warmth and truly celebrate Christmas this Christmas. •

Personal Reflections

- What was a moment when you missed Christmas?
- What are two ways you can find Christmas today?
- How can you help others find Christmas this Advent?

Hymn of Response

HARK! the Herald Angels Sing

HARK! the Herald Angels sing
Glory to the new-born King!
Peace on Earth, and Mercy mild,
God and Sinners reconcil'd.

Joyful all ye Nations rise,
Join the Triumphs of the Skies;
Nature rise and worship him,
Who is born at Bethlehem.

Christ by highest Heav'n ador'd,
Christ the everlasting Lord;
Late in Time behold-him come,
Offspring of the Virgin's Womb.

Veil'd in Flesh the Godhead see,
Hail th' incarnate Deity!
Pleas'd as Man with Men t'appear,
Jesus our Immanuel here.

Hail the Heav'n-born Prince of Peace
Hail the Sun of Righteousness!

Light and Life around he brings,
Ris'n with Healing in his Wings.

Mild he lays his Glory by,
Born that Men no more may die;
Born to raise the Sons of Earth,
Born to give them second Birth.

Come, Desire of Nations, come,
Fix in us thy heav'nly Home;
Rise the Woman's conqu'ring Seed,
Bruise in us the Serpent's Head.

Adam's Likeness now efface,
Stamp thy Image in its Place;
Second Adam from above,
Work it in us by thy Love

HARK! the Herald Angels sing
Glory to the new-born King!
Peace on Earth, and Mercy mild,
God and Sinners reconcil'd.

—written by Charles Wesley (1739);
—modified by George Whitfield (1754)

December 4

The Wonder of the Incarnation

(excerpts from Oration 45)
St. Gregory Nazianzen (329–390)
(Translated by Charles Gordon Brown and James Edward Swallow)
(Adapted by Brandon Anthony Shuman)

The Wonder of the Incarnation

The Word of God Himself, Who is before all worlds. The Invisible. The Incomprehensible. The Incorporeal. The Beginning of beginning. The Light of light. The Source of Life and Immortality. The Image of the Archetype. The Immovable Seal. The Unchangeable Image.

The Father's Definition and Word, came to His own Image, and took on Him Flesh for the sake of our flesh. He mingled Himself with an intelligent soul for my soul's sake, purifying like by like; and in all points except sin was made Man. Conceived by the Virgin, who first in body and soul was purified by the Holy Ghost, for it was needful both

That Child-bearing should be honored and that Virginity should receive a higher honor. He came forth then, as God, with That which He had assumed. One Person in Two natures, Flesh and Spirit, of which the latter deified the former. O new commingling! O strange conjunction! The Self-existent comes into Being. The Uncreated is created. That which cannot be contained is contained by the intervention of an intellectual soul mediating between the Deity and the corporeity of the flesh.

And He who gives riches becomes poor. For He assumes the poverty of my flesh, that I may assume the riches of His Godhead. He that is full empties Himself. For He empties Himself of His Glory for a short while, that I may have a share in His Fullness.

What are the riches of His Goodness? What is this mystery that is around me? I had a share in the Image, yet I did not keep it. He partakes of my flesh that He may both save the Image and make the flesh immortal. He communicates a Second Communion that is far more marvelous than the first!

Humanity must be sanctified by the Humanity of God. He delivers us Himself, and overcomes the tyrant. He draws us to Himself by the mediation of His Son, Who also arranged this to the honor of the Father, Whom it is manifest that He obeys in all things

The Good Shepherd—He who lays down His life for the sheep—came upon the mountains and hills upon which you used to sacrifice, and found the wandering one. And having found it, took it upon His shoulders, on which He also bore the wood; and having borne it, brought it back to the life above. And having brought it back to Heaven, He numbered it among those who have never strayed.

The Light that is exceedingly bright should follow the Candle—the Forerunner. The Word follows the Voice. The Bridegroom follows His friend who prepared for the Lord a peculiar people and cleansed them by the water in preparation for the Spirit.

We needed an Incarnate God—a God put to death, that we might live. We were put to death together with Him, that we might be cleansed. We rose again with Him because we were put to death with Him. We were glorified with Him because we rose again with Him. ●

December 5

Babel or Bethlehem

"The central miracle asserted by Christians is the Incarnation. They say that God became Man. Every other miracle prepares for this, or exhibits this, or results from this."

—C.S. Lewis (1898–1963), *Miracles*

"We cannot approach this manger as we approach the cradle of any other child. But who would go to this manger goes where something will happen. When he leaves the manger, he leaves either condemned or delivered. Here, he will be broken in pieces or know the compassion of God ..."

—Dietrich Bonhoeffer (1906–1945),
sermon from December 17, 1933

Jesus said to him, "I am the way, the truth, and the life. No one comes to the Father except through Me."

—John 14:6

Babel or Bethlehem

A ll roads do not lead to Rome. Instead, whether we realize it or not, all our journeys terminate in one of two places. All roads lead to Babel or Bethlehem. There are no other destinations. Every traveler's steps take them nearer to one of these two ends.

Inward and hidden is the nature of our journey, but its consequences are external and profound. Each of our thoughts and all our actions bring us one step further along a path towards one of these two cities. In the end, we will all ascend the proudest tower or bow before the humblest manger.

Drawn to image are those treading the roads to Babel. Sparkling spectacles bedazzle and transfix our eyes. Boasting gongs overwhelm and echo in our ringing ears. Lofty arguments captivate our minds. Upon its descending roads, we are mesmerized by the appearance of an object soaring from the earth. Its silhouette stains the horizon, eclipsing the sun. Its shadow stretches for miles and extends into our hearts. The image before us lures our being with aspiring promises of self, and we believe. A dense fog encloses our hearts as we approach the city of grey. At each step, our greatness swells from within until at last we reach the base of the staggering tower. A sign posted above the entrance reads, "Only look up. Never look down." After a moment's hesitation, we take hold of its promise and our foot falls loosely on the first step of the steep spire. Immediately, we are encouraged by the magnificence of our accomplishment, and we continue our ascent. Further and further, higher and higher we climb, with each step heavier and bolder than the last.

Step after empty step, we cling to the image and its promise. Glancing toward heaven and our goal, we are disheartened that the end now seems farther away than ever before. But upward, we stubbornly climb. How many hours; how many days; how many years, decades, and lifetimes pass? And always, we take one more step up the spire.

Until finally, at the end of our strength, without heart to move, we pause. Overcome by dizzying heights, we must take stock of our achievement to renew our strength for further heights above, and we break Babel's command and bow our gaze toward the earth far beneath us. The sight is stunning. The city is completely beyond our vision. Nothing but fog and clouds surround the lonely tower. Transfixed between heaven and earth, the view is exactly the same as what rises above us. How far have we come? How far to go?

Adjusting, our eyes regain perspective. We collapse at the realization. The ground beneath us is nothing but a mirror. There is no structure, no tower, no staircase at all. Everything is an illusion. Swirling sands of earth sting our eyes as we succumb to blindness. The bitter memory of our majestic tower composed of shadow and looking glass is all that remain. Upon the road to Babel, we not only lose sight of what is true, but we lose the ability to see truth at all. In the land of fleeting images, words lose their comprehension, and all meaning is lost.

Seeking the Word made flesh are those treading the road to Bethlehem. Darkness and quiet fill the landscape. A lonely star of hope occupies the night sky, but its rays illuminate our path kindling our hearts with warmth. A serene setting beckons us towards new life. Its invitation is peace on earth and good will to men. Upon its rocky road we travel, in hope of eternal healing. Within its walls we find refuge and harmony as we rest in the hope of salvation. In Bethlehem, the Word looked down, lifted up our souls and gave life a new and everlasting meaning. At the manger in Bethlehem, we access God—the manger where the Savior of the world lay. For it is in this city that Christ came to man. Here, Heaven miraculously was born on earth and with it, humble love was born in the hearts of all those who believe. The message of the manger cannot be fully recognized until we see within its shadow, cast from the radiant star against dirty stable walls, the image of the cross.

There are no towers to be made by man that will ever exalt us from earth to heaven. There is only a manger signifying Heaven's advent upon the earth. But with it is the sacrifice of a cross and an empty grave's promise to transform Heaven within us now and the divine hope that earth will one day have its eternal advent in Heaven.

Christmas is either the most ridiculous absurdity or the most wondrous miracle. The miracle of Christmas does not make sense, yet nothing in our world makes sense without Christmas. Without Christmas, everything is Babel. For scoffers in Babel, Christmas is an absurd myth and an offense to reason. For believers in Bethlehem, Christmas is not only the greatest of all miracles, but it is the miracle upon which all other miracles, reason, images, and words draw their significance. ●

Personal Reflections

- **How do you know when you are on the road to Babel?**
- **How do you know when you are on the road to Bethlehem?**

Hymn of Response

O Little Town of Bethlehem

O little town of Bethlehem
How still we see thee lie
Above thy deep and dreamless sleep
The silent stars go by
Yet in thy dark streets shineth
The everlasting Light
The hopes and fears of all the years
Are met in thee tonight

For Christ is born of Mary
And gathered all above
While mortals sleep, the angels keep
Their watch of wondering love
O morning stars together
Proclaim the holy birth
And praises sing to God the King
And Peace to men on earth

How silently, how silently
The wondrous gift is given!
So God imparts to human hearts

The blessings of His heaven.
No ear may hear His coming,
But in this world of sin,
Where meek souls will receive him still,
The dear Christ enters in.

O holy Child of Bethlehem
Descend to us, we pray
Cast out our sin and enter in
Be born to us today
We hear the Christmas angels
The great glad tidings tell
O come to us, abide with us
Our Lord Immanuel

—Philip Brooks, (1868)

December 6

An Interlude of Psalms

Psalm 2

Why do the nations rage,
And the people plot a vain thing?
The kings of the earth set themselves,
And the rulers take counsel together,
Against the Lord and against His Anointed, saying,
"Let us break Their bonds in pieces
And cast away Their cords from us."
He who sits in the heavens shall laugh;
The Lord shall hold them in derision.
Then He shall speak to them in His wrath,
And distress them in His deep displeasure:
"Yet I have set My King
On My holy hill of Zion."
"I will declare the decree:
The Lord has said to Me,
'You are My Son,
Today I have begotten You.
Ask of Me, and I will give You
The nations for Your inheritance,
And the ends of the earth for Your possession.
You shall break them with a rod of iron;
You shall dash them to pieces like a potter's vessel.'"

Now therefore, be wise, O kings;
Be instructed, you judges of the earth.
Serve the Lord with fear,
And rejoice with trembling.
Kiss the Son, lest He be angry,
And you perish in the way,
When His wrath is kindled but a little.
Blessed are all those who put their trust in Him.

Psalm 110

The Lord said to my Lord,
"Sit at My right hand,
Till I make Your enemies Your footstool."
The Lord shall send the rod of Your strength out of Zion.
Rule in the midst of Your enemies!
Your people shall be volunteers
In the day of Your power;
In the beauties of holiness, from the womb of the morning,
You have the dew of Your youth.
The Lord has sworn
And will not relent,
"You are a priest forever
According to the order of Melchizedek."
The Lord is at Your right hand;
He shall execute kings in the day of His wrath.
He shall judge among the nations,
He shall fill the places with dead bodies,
He shall execute the heads of many countries.
He shall drink of the brook by the wayside;
Therefore He shall lift up the head.

December 7

Immanuel's Song

"And when the Lord Jesus has become your peace, remember, there is another thing: good will towards men. Do not try to keep Christmas without good will towards men."

—Charles Spurgeon (1834–1892),
"The First Christmas Carol," a sermon

"The Almighty appeared on earth as a helpless human baby, unable to do more than lie and stare and wriggle, and make noises, needing to be fed and changed and taught to talk like any other child. The more you think about it, the more staggering it gets. Nothing in fiction is so fantastic as this truth of the Incarnation."

—J.I. Packer (1926–Present), *Knowing God*

The peace of God, which surpasses all understanding, will guard your hearts and minds through Christ Jesus.

—Philippians 4:7

Immanuel's Song

O f all the world's longings, the ember that burns deepest in the human heart is peace. Peace is the fullest measure by which we gauge the wellness of the world. Peace is a state of wholeness, free from any antagonistic division or strife. Peace is the transcendent craving of every man, woman, and child. Peace is the hopeful song of every soul who has ever lived, yet the human voice is harsh, discordant, and out of tune. True peace is a harmonious melody unsung by mortal choirs whose notes are beyond the human range to intonate. Tragic and strange is it not, that peace should be so highly esteemed by creatures whose condition is wickedness and enmity? In our fallen irony, we skillfully innovate bitterness, covetousness, worry, and war, often in the pursuit of peace, and the thing we want most is that which we cannot acquire.

From the moment we left Eden, our long, burdensome history has been one of perpetual war. The term *peace* merely describes the occasional interlude to this sad saga. In an effort to escape our predicament, some have placed their faith in human wisdom to discover a solution and entrusted its establishment to the inherent goodness of man. But history is littered with plastic kingdoms and paper treaties, which are all fabrications of the Pax Romana—the misguided vision that enduring harmony can be manufactured by human strength or government. The results of such "peace" are hollow at best and unspeakable at their worst. Though our problems are man-made, they cannot be solved by man alone; thus, peace has become an empty promise, unable to materialize. Others have tempered their expectations by ill-defining peace to mean no more than the absence of hostility. Proclamations of "Peace! Peace!" when there is no peace have been infamously declared since the days of Jeremiah. But ignoring reality changes nothing and only leads to further conflict with truth. Neither path alleviates our souls. One erects our greatest hopes upon sandy foundations of on short-sighted and deeply flawed assumptions; the other buries its head in sand, substituting undeniable values for self-deceiving apathy. And so peace has become a relative, shallow term without substance, meaning, or flavor.

With the most elusive and stubborn of human desires unattainable, formless and void, peace came to our peace-less world in the most unthinkable of ways. Rising from a manager, hovering in the crisp air, the cries of a baby making His first sounds burst forth on a dark Bethlehem night, and the Prince of Peace was born. God had come near. By His sheer presence, what was empty and without form was recreated and filled. By His proximity alone, the true definition of peace was reinstated: Immanuel, God with us. Peace is not merely a lack or an absence. Peace divinely understood is overflowing with the presence of God.

At Advent, Immanuel traversed dimensions of eternity and immaterial to bring us peace in the course of human events—in the only way it could possibly be received—by giving us Himself. Christ has returned to Heaven in preparation of our everlasting advent, but His presence among us is evergreen. The fullness of Christmas is not therefore, the awesome yet bare recognition of God's presence in human affairs two thousand years ago; rather, Christmas is our personal experience of Immanuel's presence within our lives now.

Peace, like hope and joy, and selfless acts of love depend upon the reality of divine foundations. While our external wish for peace on earth eagerly awaits His second coming, we rejoice in the inner peace of our reconciliation to God. Immanuel's peace extends far beyond superficial circumstance and reaches into the haunted chambers of our souls, surpassing every doubt and fear of our understanding to satisfy the deepest aches of our hearts. By coming to earth, God demonstrated His good will, by His stripes we have been healed, by His death all enmity between heaven and our souls has been abolished, and by His resurrection, God established a lasting and indwelling peace for all who abide in Him. God has given us new notes to sing and added human voices to heavenly music. By His grace, may we too, lend our voices in harmony with angelic choirs this Christmas and sing songs of peace—the song "God With Us"—the song of Immanuel.

"Glory to God in the highest, and on earth peace, goodwill to men!" ●

Personal Reflections

● What is an area or relationship of your life that lacks peace—the kind that overflows with God's presence?

● Ask God to calm your heart with the fullness of His presence.

● How can your life proclaim Immanuel today?

Hymn of Response

Silent Night

Silent night, holy night,
All is calm, all is bright
Round yon virgin mother and child.
Holy infant, so tender and mild,
Sleep in heavenly peace,
Sleep in heavenly peace.

Silent night, holy night,
Shepherds quake at the sight;
Glories stream from heaven afar,
Heavenly hosts sing Alleluia!
Christ the Savior is born,
Christ the Savior is born!

Silent night, holy night,
Son of God, love's pure light;
Radiant beams from thy holy face
With the dawn of redeeming grace,
Jesus, Lord, at thy birth,
Jesus, Lord, at thy birth.

—Joseph Mohr (German) (1818)
—music Franz Xaver Gruber (1818)
—translated John Freeman Young (1859)

December 8

The House of Bread

"By taking flesh, God did not lessen His majesty;
and in consequence did not lessen the reason for
reverencing Him, which is increased by the increase
of knowledge of Him. But, on the contrary, inasmuch
as He wished to draw nigh to us by taking flesh, He
greatly drew us to know Him."

—St. Thomas Aquinas (1225–1274), *Summa Theologica*

"The arc of the moral universe is long, but it bends
toward Justice."

—Dr. Martin Luther King Jr. (1929–1968)

As the deer pants for the water brooks,
So pants my soul for You, O God.

—Psalm 42:1

The threshing floors shall be full of wheat,
And the vats shall overflow with new wine and oil.

—Joel 2:24

The House of Bread

As creatures of earth, we are humbled by small horizons. Finite and frail, we are omni-dependent upon the most basic of needs. Indeed, we cannot sustain our lives beyond a moment without our lungs breathing life-giving air. Our organs dry and perish without the constant replenishment of water, and our bodies wither and lose their strength without the sustained nourishment of food. We are all beggars in need.

God in His goodness hath given us air to fill our lungs; water to quicken our lips; and bread to strengthen our bodies. The world is full of life-giving manna. We thank God for providing our daily bread, but a deeper hunger persists. Its cravings never cease. Its pangs never subside. Despite the abundance of food, nothing satisfies its rumblings.

There is a passionate need for justice, a longing for wrongs to be righted, and an abiding cry for satisfaction. There is a wrenching within our souls for righteousness. The world is starving. Cursed by an unrelenting famine, the brooks of mercy run dry. The harvests of harmony are meager. The threshing floors of righteousness are full of tares, and the grain stores of shalom are bare.

To where can we turn for justice?

Even at their best, our courts with a hundred Solomons as their judges are incapable of rendering wholeness to even the simplest matter. Our highest wisdom and best virtues cannot bring the wholeness we seek. Human justice approaches the case from afar. Its superficial applications never fully restore. Such "justice" is only a gesture reminding us of what ought to be but never is. There is brokenness that cannot be mended. There are hurts that cannot be healed, and no recompense we pay can undo sin or eliminate its miserable wake.

The wicked prosper and the righteous perish. Justice has forsaken our lands. In its place, corruption plagues our towns. Violence fills our streets. Treachery lurks within our homes. Deceit dwells in our hearts. The adversary has bribed our judges and intimidated our juries, but we are not merely his victims, as we have been enlisted into his schemes. We are complicit in his crimes. We have become the unjust and the doers of evil. Like devouring locusts, sin eats the crop of righteousness and strips harmony's leaves. Everything is wasted. In their desolate condition, communities tear apart. Lacking goodness, our famished society turns against itself and fails us in our time of need.

The tables we set are bare. The banquets we host ring hollow. The feasts we serve do not satisfy. The bread of righteousness is molding. The cup of justice is empty as the bitter cups of injustice are brimming and overspill.

Famished. Hungry. Alone. Our days are marked by one appalling travesty after another. The very earth hungers and groans for its day of redemption. Whence can we turn for justice? Where are its tables that we may sit and dine? Is there any food to nourish our dying souls? Is there no house left undimmed by sin?

There is but one place where Justice abides. There is but one table where its life-giving bread is served. There is but one house where the righteous find rest. It is called "Bethlehem: The House of Bread." At Christmas, it was to Bethlehem, the House of Bread, that Jesus Christ, the Bread of Heaven, was given unto us.

Christ is the only food to be eaten. Jesus is the only satisfaction we can enjoy. The only life we have is in Him. Only in Christ will all wrongs be made right. Only in Him will we be made full and restored. In Bethlehem is Christ—our Righteousness—found. It is in a manger—a humble feeding trough for the lowest of creatures—that the Bread of Heaven is served. Upon this lowly table, God and man commune.

Bethlehem's banquet is simple. Its table serves but one meal. Its invitation goes to all, but how few attend? For only those who starve for a righteousness not their own are able to enter in and be filled. Far from the palaces of the proud, behind the crowded rooms of an inn, is where Christ is born. It is in this stable that those who have renounced themselves for the sake of Jesus find themselves. This Christmas, and every day into eternity, the humble and the hungry feast in Bethlehem.

So, let us go to the House of Bread and be filled. Even now, our Savior is knocking at our heart's door. We need only to listen to his voice and open to receive Christmas' greatest gift—Christ Himself, Heaven's Bread. As we eat the body, broken for us, our souls are nourished to fullness and health. In this house, our hearts find both forgiveness and the strength to forgive. At the table of grace, we have grace in abundance to enjoy and share eternally. In Bethlehem, we find not only Justice—the rightness of all things; we share Shalom—the prosperity of all things in perfect harmony when they fully become themselves.

When we receive Heaven's Bread through faith, His righteousness becomes our righteousness. His life becomes our life. His love becomes our love. As we live in Him, we love the world as He loves the world—the world He was given to save, the world ever groaning for the sons of righteousness to be revealed. Like our Just and Gracious Savior, who freely gave His life and body to be broken that we might eat and live, we die to ourselves as sacrificial grains that fall upon the earth so others might taste and see the goodness of God. Like our Savior, we rise again to new life.

Because of Bethlehem, we consider not only what is just for ourselves but what is good for others. Like our Savior before us, we regard our rights as not something to be asserted or attained. We, like Jesus, humble ourselves through obedience. We offer our lives and empty them in Him so that others may be filled. Our lives are invitations to others to partake at Bethlehem's table—to the manger—to where the Heavenly Bread is eternally given for all who hunger for righteousness. This Christmas, let us come to the banquet in Bethlehem and enjoy fellowship together with our Lord. Amen. ●

Personal Reflections

- What food are your feeding your soul?
- In your daily life, how do you partake of Jesus's offer? "This is my body broken for you. Take. Eat. All of it."

Hymn of Response

O Bread of Life from Heaven

O Bread of Life from Heaven,
O Food to pilgrims given,
O Manna from above:
Feed with the blessed sweetness
Of Your divine completeness
The souls that want and need Your love.

O Fount of grace redeeming,
O River ever streaming,
From Jesus' wounded side:
Come now, Your love bestowing
On thirsting souls, and flowing
Till all are fully satisfied.

We love You, Jesus, tender,
In all Your hidden splendor
Within these means of grace.
Oh, let the veil be riven,
And our clear eye in Heaven
Behold Your glory face to face."

—17th Century German Hymn
—Translated by John Athelstan Laurie Riley (1906)

December 9

What Virgil Knew

"Eclogue IV" by the Roman Poet
Virgil (70 B.C.–19 B.C.)
(translated by William Blake)

The Roman poet, Virgil, lived during the worst of times and the best of times. He endured the tumult and upheaval of three civil wars and saw the rise of Caesar Augustus, and enjoyed the prosperity under his reign—Rome's first golden age. His masterpiece was *The Aeneid*. Recasting the mythology of Homer and interweaving them with historical Roman events, Virgil wrote an epic praising the glory of Rome.

But Virgil also wrote other poetry, including the *Eclogues*, a series of landscape and poetry honoring the beauty of nature and agriculture. But in his fourth eclogue, Virgil sings a "loftier" tune. His subject is the praise of a new age soon to come, "when circling centuries begin anew," when "Justice returns . . . with a new breed of men sent down from heaven," when a divine child is born unto "tottering" world longing for the life he will give it. Unsurprisingly, *Eclogue IV* has been called the "Messianic Eclogue."

How peculiar that a pagan, Roman poet would write such lines, many of which could conceivably be mistaken for the prophecies of Isaiah. It is all the more interesting that Virgil concludes *Eclogue IV* by lamenting that if his days would be prolonged just a little bit longer, he too would see this coming child and no one would out-praise him with poetry. Virgil died in 19 B.C.

Did God pull back the curtain and give this pagan poet a glimpse into things to come? Was Virgil a kind of prophet to the Romans, who uttered unto them in darkness the good things he dimly foresaw? Was Virgil to Rome what the Magi were to the Persians? God speaks in mysterious ways. ●

Eclogue IV

POLLIO

Muses of Sicily, essay we now
A somewhat loftier task! Not all men love
Coppice or lowly tamarisk: sing we woods,
Woods worthy of a Consul let them be.
Now the last age by Cumae's Sibyl sung
Has come and gone, and the majestic roll
Of circling centuries begins anew:
Justice returns, returns old Saturn's reign,
With a new breed of men sent down from heaven.
Only do thou, at the boy's birth in whom
The iron shall cease, the golden race arise,
Befriend him, chaste Lucina; 'tis thine own
Apollo reigns. And in thy consulate,
This glorious age, O Pollio, shall begin,
And the months enter on their mighty march.
Under thy guidance, whatso tracks remain
Of our old wickedness, once done away,

Shall free the earth from never-ceasing fear.
He shall receive the life of gods, and see
Heroes with gods commingling, and himself
Be seen of them, and with his father's worth
Reign o'er a world at peace. For thee, O boy,
First shall the earth, untilled, pour freely forth
Her childish gifts, the gadding ivy-spray
With foxglove and Egyptian bean-flower mixed,
And laughing-eyed acanthus. Of themselves,
Untended, will the she-goats then bring home
Their udders swollen with milk, while flocks afield
Shall of the monstrous lion have no fear.
Thy very cradle shall pour forth for thee
Caressing flowers. The serpent too shall die,
Die shall the treacherous poison-plant, and far
And wide Assyrian spices spring. But soon
As thou hast skill to read of heroes' fame,
And of thy father's deeds, and inly learn
What virtue is, the plain by slow degrees
With waving corn-crops shall to golden grow,
From the wild briar shall hang the blushing grape,
And stubborn oaks sweat honey-dew. Nathless
Yet shall there lurk within of ancient wrong
Some traces, bidding tempt the deep with ships,
Gird towns with walls, with furrows cleave the earth.
Therewith a second Tiphys shall there be,
Her hero-freight a second Argo bear;
New wars too shall arise, and once again
Some great Achilles to some Troy be sent.
Then, when the mellowing years have made thee man,
No more shall mariner sail, nor pine-tree bark
Ply traffic on the sea, but every land
Shall all things bear alike: the glebe no more
Shall feel the harrow's grip, nor vine the hook;
The sturdy ploughman shall loose yoke from steer,

Nor wool with varying colours learn to lie;
But in the meadows shall the ram himself,
Now with soft flush of purple, now with tint
Of yellow saffron, teach his fleece to shine.
While clothed in natural scarlet graze the lambs.
"Such still, such ages weave ye, as ye run,"
Sang to their spindles the consenting Fates
By Destiny's unalterable decree.
Assume thy greatness, for the time draws nigh,
Dear child of gods, great progeny of Jove!
See how it totters- the world's orbed might,
Earth, and wide ocean, and the vault profound,
All, see, enraptured of the coming time!
Ah! might such length of days to me be given,
And breath suffice me to rehearse thy deeds,
Nor Thracian Orpheus should out-sing me then,
Nor Linus, though his mother this, and that
His sire should aid- Orpheus Calliope,
And Linus fair Apollo. Nay, though Pan,
With Arcady for judge, my claim contest,
With Arcady for judge great Pan himself
Should own him foiled, and from the field retire.
Begin to greet thy mother with a smile,
O baby-boy! ten months of weariness
For thee she bore: O baby-boy, begin!
For him, on whom his parents have not smiled,
Gods deem not worthy of their board or bed.

December 10

The Moment of Christmas

"Bethlehem is emphatically a place where extremes meet."

—G.K. Chesterton (1874–1936), *The Everlasting Man*

"We must both read and meditate upon the nativity. If the meditation does not reach the heart, we shall sense no sweetness, nor shall we know what solace for humankind lies in the contemplation. The heart will not laugh nor be merry. As spray does not touch the deep, so mere meditation will not quiet the heart. There is such richness and goodness in this nativity that if we should see and deeply understand, we should be dissolved in perpetual joy."

—Martin Luther (1483–1546), "Annunciation"
(*as quoted by Roland Herbert Bainton in Martin Luther's Christmas Book*)

"Vanity of vanities," says the Preacher;
"Vanity of vanities, all is vanity."

—Ecclesiastes 1:2

The Moment of Christmas

God has placed eternity in the hearts of men, yet we toil each moment of our lives under the sun. We all experience moments of gladness and mirth, but for every occasion to be merry, there are dozens for drudgery, sickness, and sorrow. Beneath the sun, we laugh and we cry; we suffer; we hope and dream; we pray, we seek justice, and we love. We strive to make something better of ourselves and our world. Under the sun, we look toward the future while clinging to our past. We remember who we are supposed to be while we forget what we are. We build, we destroy, we rebuild; we gain, we lose; we scatter and gather; we begin and end wars; we speak and we are silent.

We dissipate each moment of our lives in the pursuit of something elusively higher, or in the futile struggle to maintain our uneasy oblivion to its existence. Regardless of every feeling screaming inside us, in spite of every action futilely asserting otherwise, our deepest fear is confirmed: everything is vanity.

All of us are born under the sun, and under the sun, all of us will die.

All our moments come to an end. Death has impatiently lingered for our moments to conclude since the days of Adam. One day soon, death will snatch us from our loved ones just as it has stolen those we love from us. Death has no cure. There is no drug to disremember our longing for eternity. We cannot get out from underneath the sun. Our souls are trapped beneath its rays and wither in its heat. We are locked in the temporal with only a recollection of the eternal, bound upon earth with a burning desire for heaven. There is not a moment in our lives where we are free to breathe eternal air.

None of our actions—however passionate, however high, or however strong—are enough to teach our spirits to fly beyond gravity's chains. Every action, every dream, and every moment of every life was doomed to die that fatal moment sin entered the world and laid waste our souls.

Thus was life under the sun.

Thus was the world . . . until, the fullness of time when God sent forth His Son, born of a woman under the law, to redeem those under the law, so that they—so that *we*—might receive adoption as sons. Christmas is the moment of divine love when God left Heaven to enter our world under the sun, giving His only begotten Son so that whosoever believes in Him shall not perish but have everlasting life. Until that moment, all was lost. Since that moment, all things are being made new.

Christmas changed everything. When man could not ascend to God, God came to man. When we could not reach Heaven, Heaven reached down and touched our souls and lit the candle of our hearts on fire. With all our moments fading like a whisper in time, the Eternal Word became flesh and dwelt among us. With our hearts bleeding for life while beating ever closer to death, a Heavenly babe was born under Bethlehem skies to die so that in Him we might profit and live.

The moment of Christmas is God's love for us. Christmas is the moment we breathe Heavenly air. Christmas is the moment we are made whole and our souls take flight. Christmas is the moment our hearts must no longer pine for eternity, waiting to die; but when they cross the thresholds of death and time into life-everlasting. Christmas becomes every moment we redeem for eternity, giving to others the same love He gave to us. Christmas is love's enduring moment.

Because of Christmas, who we are and what we do are no longer reduced to vanity. The Christmas moment changed everything under the sun. Because of that moment, we can forever rejoice! ●

Personal Reflections

- ● **How would your life be different without Christmas?**
- ● **Do others see this difference in you?**

Hymn of Response

O Holy Night

O holy night, the stars are brightly shining,
It is the night of the dear Saviour's birth;
Long lay the world in sin and error pining,
'Till he appeared and the soul felt its worth.
A thrill of hope the weary world rejoices,
For yonder breaks a new and glorious morn;

Fall on your knees, Oh hear the angel voices!
O night divine! O night when Christ was born.
O night, O holy night, O night divine.

Led by the light of Faith serenely beaming;
With glowing hearts by his cradle we stand:
So, led by light of a star sweetly gleaming,
Here come the wise men from Orient land,
The King of Kings lay thus in lowly manger,
In all our trials born to be our friend;

He knows our need, To our weakness no stranger!
Behold your King! Before Him lowly bend!
Behold your King! your King! before him bend!

Truly He taught us to love one another;
His law is Love and His gospel is Peace;
Chains shall he break, for the slave is our brother,
And in his name all oppression shall cease,
Sweet hymns of joy in grateful Chorus raise we;
Let all within us praise his Holy name!

Christ is the Lord, then ever! ever praise we!
His pow'r and glory, evermore proclaim!
His pow'r and glory, evermore proclaim

Fall on your knees, Oh hear the angel voices!
O night divine! O night when Christ was born.
O night, O holy night, O night divine.

—Placide Cappeau, (French) (1843);
—Music Adophe Adam (1847);
—translated John Sullivan Dwight (1855)

December 11

Scriptural Interlude: The Magnificat & Nativity

The Magnificat: Luke 1:47–55

And Mary said:
"My soul magnifies the Lord,
And my spirit has rejoiced in God my Savior.
For He has regarded the lowly state of His maidservant;
For behold, henceforth all generations will call me blessed.
For He who is mighty has done great things for me,
And holy is His name.
And His mercy is on those who fear Him
From generation to generation.
He has shown strength with His arm;
He has scattered the proud in the imagination of their hearts.
He has put down the mighty from their thrones,
And exalted the lowly.
He has filled the hungry with good things,
And the rich He has sent away empty.
He has helped His servant Israel,
In remembrance of His mercy,
As He spoke to our fathers,
To Abraham and to his seed forever."

The Birth of Christ: Luke 2:1–20

And it came to pass in those days that a decree went out from Caesar Augustus that all the world should be registered. This census first took place while Quirinius was governing Syria. So all went to be registered, everyone to his own city.

Joseph also went up from Galilee, out of the city of Nazareth, into Judea, to the city of David, which is called Bethlehem, because he was of the house and lineage of David, to be registered with Mary, his betrothed wife, who was with child. So it was, that while they were there, the days were completed for her to be delivered. And she brought forth her firstborn Son, and wrapped Him in swaddling cloths, and laid Him in a manger, because there was no room for them in the inn.

Now there were in the same country shepherds living out in the fields, keeping watch over their flock by night. And behold, an angel of the Lord stood before them, and the glory of the Lord shone around them, and they were greatly afraid. Then the angel said to them, "Do not be afraid, for behold, I bring you good tidings of great joy which will be to all people. For there is born to you this day in the city of David a Savior, who is Christ the Lord. And this will be the sign to you: You will find a Babe wrapped in swaddling cloths, lying in a manger."

And suddenly there was with the angel a multitude of the heavenly host praising God and saying:

"Glory to God in the highest,

And on earth peace, goodwill toward men!"

So it was, when the angels had gone away from them into heaven, that the shepherds said to one another, "Let us now go to Bethlehem and see this thing that has come to pass, which the Lord has made known to us." And they came with haste and found Mary and Joseph, and the Babe lying in a manger. Now when they had seen Him, they made widely known the saying which was told them concerning this Child.

And all those who heard it marveled at those things which were told them by the shepherds. But Mary kept all these things and pondered them in her heart. Then the shepherds returned, glorifying and praising God for all the things that they had heard and seen, as it was told them.

December 12

Heaven's Joy

"Once in our world, a stable had something in it that was bigger than our whole world."

—C.S. Lewis (1898–1963), *The Last Battle*

"It is good to be children sometimes, and never better than Christmas, when its mighty Founder was a child Himself."

—Charles Dickens (1812–1870), *A Christmas Carol*

Again, the kingdom of heaven is like treasure hidden in a field, which a man found and hid; and for joy over it he goes and sells all that he has and buys that field.

—Matthew 13:44

Heaven's Joy

T he measure of a man's joy is proportional to the measure of that man's faith. The greater or smaller a man's faith, the greater or lesser his joy will be.

So it is, in this fallen world of woe, that the joyless sighs of our hearts reveal the littleness of our faith. For nothing on earth satisfies the eternity haunting our hearts.

Behind every happiness lies an ache. The very earth we trod groans for its redemption. And the days are evil. The happiness we pursue, once found, neither endure nor satisfy. Set against eternity, all our smiles are mortal, and every moment of happiness is greeted by the tragic promise that nothing lasts forever.

Like a band of thieves, a cacophony of lies overwhelm and kidnap our souls. They blindfold our vision and mute our cries until we believe only in what we are able to see. Stolen and hidden away in the dungeons of materialism, that lie becomes our reality. Our very souls forget even themselves, and joy becomes a fraudulent mentality. Leaning on our own understanding, we accept the stunted horizons of a world finite-ed by sin and death.

Having nursed on breasts of bitterness, we scoff at the man who prospects in heaven's joys, thinking him naïve and ungrounded in reality. Joy is the unbound madness of holy fools who have renounced this world. As practical men of reason, our happiness, like our faith, is safely bound to this world. Self-prudent and wise, we reject joy and congratulate ourselves for being emotionally honest.

Having exchanged our child-like faith for beliefs that are too small-minded, our wants quickly become too small-hearted to enjoy Heaven's goods. We abandon celestial joys of heaven in exchange for earthly souvenirs. Fixing our sights on these earthly treasures, our hearts ceaselessly binge on mediocrity and develop a taste for things that never satisfy. Our souls are diminished and consumed by the very things for which they frenzy. Having closed our minds to joy, our weakened hearts lose their strength to rejoice. And without joy, life, at its best, is a struggle in the search for solace amidst suffering.

Thus, we walk through life tempered because we know how temporal life can be.

We dare not surrender our demented minds from joyless lies, lest joy unhinge our thoughts. We dare not give our frail hearts to joy, lest disappointment shatter them.

In a world full of woes, it takes faith to rejoice.

Joy is birthed in the conviction that Good will ultimately triumph over evil. That Light is more lasting than darkness. That Life has defeated death. That a Baby in a manger miraculously altered the arc of eternity.

The angels' message to the shepherds of Bethlehem was that God is man's Friend and the Lover of man's soul. The shepherds' joy was their souls' leap at the wonderfulness of the most certain of things. Joy is our assurance that God's love is more powerful than all suffering. Joy is our heart's affirmation that Christ's victory over sin and death is secured. Joy is Heaven's laughter against all the sieges hell can muster. Joy is the eternal fact that God's kingdom will never be shaken. It is in the glorious light of these truest of truths that joy is our only honest response to reality unfiltered. Joy is our soul's exhilaration in the truth of Christmas.

The message of Christmas is one of everlasting joy. Christmas is joy's proclamation that a Savior has come to earth to set the captives free. Christmas is joy's redemption of our evil days. Christmas is joy's promise that Heaven is eternally given unto all who have faith to believe in Jesus' name.

Do we have faith to believe these truest of truths?

All of eternity is packed into Christmas. Christmas is eternity's choice, and we cannot be citizens of two kingdoms. It is here at Bethlehem, in a stable, beside a manger that we must choose whether or not we will receive its joys. Earth is not wide enough to hold even the smallest of Heaven's joys. And Heaven's radiance outshines the brightest luster of earth's most cherished consolations. If we are to participate in the happiness of God's kingdom this Christmas, we must hope beyond mortal horizons. We must have our hearts enlarged. We must increase our faith. So let us celebrate the marvelous gift of our Savior, and let us receive Him with an abiding Joy.

"Let us rejoice in the Lord always. Again I say, 'Rejoice!'" ●

Personal Reflections

- What does your joy indicate about the measure of your faith?
- What earthly consolations restrain your joy?
- What doubts or fears limit your faith?
- Pray the desperate father's prayer,

  "I believe, Lord! Help my unbelief."

Hymn of Response

Joy to the World

Joy to the World; the Lord is come!
Let earth receive her King!
Let ev'ry heart prepare Him room,
And Heaven and nature sing.

Joy to the earth, the Savior reigns!
Let men their songs employ;
While fields & floods, rocks, hills & plains
Repeat the sounding joy.

No more let sins and sorrows grow,
Nor thorns infest the ground;
He comes to make his blessings flow
Far as the curse is found.

He rules the world with truth and grace,
And makes the nations prove
The glories of His righteousness,
And wonders of His love.

—Isaac Watts (1719)

December 13

Light in the Darkness

"The joy of God goes through the poverty of the manger and the agony of the cross; that is why it is invincible, irrefutable. It does not deny the anguish, when it is there, but finds God In the midst of it, in fact precisely there; it does not deny grave sin but finds forgiveness precisely in this way; it looks death straight in the eye, but finds life precisely within it."

—Dietrich Bonhoeffer (1906–1945),
Circular Letter to Friends and Former Students, 1942

"The very purpose of Christ's coming into the world was that he might offer up his life as a sacrifice for the sins of men. He came to die. This is the heart of Christmas."

—Rev. Billy Graham (1918–2018), attributed

And God saw the light, that it was good;
And God divided the light from the darkness.

—Genesis 1:4

Light in the Darkness

"... light has come into the world, and men loved darkness
rather than the light, because their deeds were evil."

—John 3:19

The world is dark. Unspeakable atrocities and an all-too-real evil engulfs our planet. This undeniable reality is confirmed by our callous familiarity with the terms: *racism, fraud, injustice, terrorism, corruption, hacking, genocide,* and *lone gunman.* Our intimate acquaintance with the devastations wrought by recessions, furious storms, massive earthquakes, tragic accidents, cancer, disease, divorce, and suicide further testify to this sad fact. Wave after wave of anguish assault us from every direction. Calamity upon calamity. Tragedy upon tragedy. Grief upon grief. Each new day speaks of further atrocities and heinous crimes, reminding us that the world is growing darker still. Every season invites hosts of evils. No one is immune. No place is safe. There is no peace. The world is blanketed with a chilling omnipresent darkness.

"The lamp of the body is the eye ... but if your eye is bad,
your whole body will be full of darkness. If therefore the
light that is in you is darkness, how great is that darkness!"

—Matthew 6:22–23

As dark as our world is, there is a greater darkness still. Within our souls exists a blackness unfathomable. Its inward evil shuns away all light. This inescapable reality is authenticated by our own thoughts and desires. Malice. Greed. Envy. Hatred. Lust. Wrath. Arrogance. Inwardly, everyone is alone, trapped in an empty darkness with nothing but the stale crumbs of self for sustenance. The inner darkness is personal, belonging to none but ourselves. So profound is our internal night that our souls are deformed shadows, bearing none but the faintest traces of our intended selves. Our souls recoil in horror at its recognition or violently reject the hideousness of our current shape. Impotent to transform our vileness into something pure, enslaved by our own evil, we externalize our darkness and shroud the world with hatred. Amidst the broken shards of shattered souls, we confess the only place darker than the world we inhabit is the depths within our hearts that have made it so.

"The people who sat in darkness have seen a great light. And upon those who sat in the region and shadow of death, Light has dawned."

—Matthew 4:16

The reality is, we now find ourselves besieged by evil without and consumed by evil within. Against the reality of such evil that our fondest hopes are dashed and dearest dreams crushed. Encircled in the devastation of a thousand personal wars, our hearts break. We cry out from the depths as the tragic waves overwhelm and drown our voices. Alone in the void, we impatiently pray.

As our prayers echo into silence, we wait for salvation to come. Staring into the abyss, holding our breath, we wait for Heaven's healing answer, for a voice from above, for a sign in the sky. We groan for His coming. Frozen in darkness, we wait for the Light of the World.

"When they saw the star, they rejoiced with exceedingly great joy."

—Matthew 2:10

We need God's presence now more than ever. We need Immanuel. We need the Light of the World to illuminate our souls and cast out our darkness. We need the Bread of Heaven to come down and nourish our hearts and minds. We need the Prince of Peace to be birthed in our hearts. We need salvation. We need the reality of His love to replace our hate and to teach our broken souls to love one another in a broken world. We need a God who grieves our pain. For every tragedy we create or encounter, we need the grace upon grace upon grace upon grace that only God gives. We need a God who will defeat all our evil by the power of His goodness. We need a God who can reverse the abnormalities of disease and death. We need the healing touch of Jesus to restore our universe and to put back the pieces of our shattered selves into something new and beautiful. We need the reality of Christmas. ●

"In Him was life, and the life was the light of men.
And the light shines in the darkness, and the darkness
did not comprehend it."

—John 1:4–5

Personal Reflections

- ● **What depths has God saved you from?**
- ● **What depths is He still saving you from?**

Hymn of Response

O Come, O Come, Immanuel

O come, O come, Immanuel,
And ransom captive Israel,
That mourns in lonely exile here,
Until the Son of God appear.
Rejoice! Rejoice! Immanuel
Shall come to thee, O Israel.

O come, Thou Rod of Jesse, free
Thine own from Satan's tyranny;
From depths of hell Thy people save,
And give them victory o'er the grave.
Rejoice! Rejoice! Immanuel
Shall come to thee, O Israel.

O come, Thou Dayspring, from on high,
And cheer us by Thy drawing nigh;
Disperse the gloomy clouds of night,
And death's dark shadows put to flight.
Rejoice! Rejoice! Immanuel
Shall come to thee, O Israel.

O come, Thou Key of David, come
And open wide our heav'nly home;
Make safe the way that leads on high,
And close the path to misery.
Rejoice! Rejoice! Immanuel
Shall come to thee, O Israel.

O come, Adonai, Lord of might,
Who to Thy tribes, on Sinai's height,
In ancient times didst give the law
In cloud and majesty and awe.
Rejoice! Rejoice! Immanuel
Shall come to thee, O Israel.

—Latin Hymn (1710);
—translated J.M. Neale (1851);
—modified (1861)

December 14

O Come, Redeemer of the Earth

Ambrose (340–397)
(translated by J.M. Neale)

O Come, Redeemer of the Earth

O Come, Redeemer of the earth,
and manifest thy virgin-birth.
Let every age in wonder fall:
such birth befits the God of all.

Begotten of no human will
but of the Spirit, Thou art still
the Word of God in flesh arrayed,
the promised fruit to man displayed.

The Virgin's womb that burden gained,
its virgin honor still unstained.
The banners there of virtue glow;
God in his temple dwells below.

Proceeding from His chamber free
that royal home of purity

a giant in twofold substance one,
rejoicing now His course to run.

O equal to the Father, Thou!
gird on Thy fleshly mantle now;
the weakness of our mortal state
with deathless might invigorate.

Thy cradle here shall glitter bright,
and darkness breathe a newer light
where endless faith shall shine serene
and twilight never intervene.

All praise, eternal Son, to Thee,
whose advent sets Thy people free,
whom, with the Father, we adore,
and Holy Ghost, for evermore. Amen.

December 15

The Birth of Greatness

"How could God have shown his goodness in a more sublime manner than by humbling himself to partake of flesh and blood . . ."

—Martin Luther (1483–1546),
a Wartburg sermon, circa 1522

"At this Christmas when Christ comes, will He find a warm heart? Mark the season of Advent by loving and serving the others with God's own love and concern."

—Mother Teresa (1910–1997),
Love a Fruit that is Always in Season

---

*Then a dispute arose among them as to
which of them would be the greatest.*

—Luke 9:46

The Birth of Greatness

The unwavering orientation and ultimate aspiration of our lives is greatness. This impulse is woven into the very ether of our souls. Man was made to be great. Before the sixth dawn, our Creator declared the world "*good.*" Then the earth's dust was breathed to life, and by evening's setting sun, creation was "*very good.*" Yet, the symphony remained incomplete. God's intent was for His image-bearers to join Him in divine collaboration to perfect the masterpiece by becoming great.

But greatness never came.

When our first ancestors believed the lie, our destiny was disabled. Greatness lingered as an untapped potential. Sin's seismic shock re-magnetized our senses. Our drive for greatness remained intact, but our direction was disoriented.

For all our insecurities and striving for significance, we have little concept of what greatness is. Only fragments of its forgotten memory remain. Without this notion, all is lost. In a world defined by failure and mediocrity, we mis-define the one term, that in turn, determines the very measure of our lives.

Under fallen influence, we have continued to pursue our lost destiny. We have built civilizations out of wilderness, transfigured grain into bread, pressed grapes into wine, but we have no science or art to transfigure ourselves. We have no wisdom to redeem dust into starlight. Our best accomplishments only approach the semblance of greatness, but no one has glimpsed its form.

More disturbing still, our worst actions poison what little good we seemingly achieve. Avarice twists our best impulses only to steal, kill, and destroy. Acedia casts down our souls into a depressed, loveless apathy. Inaction in the face of evil and buried talents yields only further bitterness and shame. No artistic splendor or technological wonder in history could ever atone for the selfish wars we daily wage in vainglorious pursuit of superiority over our fellow man.

Such is the heritage of our race and our individual lives. Our self-exalting selves have thoroughly instituted a toxic definition for greatness that spoils everything sacred. Through endless successions of Alexanders and Herods, greatness has come to mean the coercive power of one misguided soul extracting what it pleases against the free will of another. As proud men, we cannot abide greatness because our hearts are too small to fathom its worth.

For Greatness is not the proud stuff of power or prestige; Greatness is the humility of mangers and crosses.

Greatness was first born when God entered the stables of our hopeless humanity. In forsaking heaven for earth, Christ did not merely transform the world to suit His liking. He did not make it appropriate for a cosmic King. Rather He emptied Himself of every royal right and came amidst all our inappropriateness, divinely wearing all our frailties, hurts, and fears. In a manger, God met humanity on its own terms.

In Christ, the semblance and form of Greatness became flesh. When He had grown in wisdom and stature, the One who was manger-born gloriously demonstrated that greatness is not lording it over others; it is loving people through humble acts of service. His life was greatness unfathomed, and His greatness unfolded right before humanity's wonder-starved eyes. Overcoming every temptation, in humble obedience to His Father—even unto death on a cross—Christ received the name that is above all names, and He taught breathing dust to shine with Him like forever-stars.

Because of Christmas and the cross, greatness is ever before us if we humble ourselves to serve. Greatness is found inside the mangers and upon the crosses God presents us every day. Mangers are the means by which we make ourselves available to love those with whom we live or encounter. They are the portals whereby we humbly are born into another's world amidst the darkness of their hurts and fears with only waxing candles for hope. Crosses are the instruments whereby we humbly set aside our earthly ambition and die for the sacrificial good of another. Crosses are the means by which we show no greater love.

Greatness is in humility. Greatness is through serving. Greatness is love. Of all mighty actions, the greatest is love. Love is the paradox of greatness. Nothing is more mundane or ordinary; nothing more adventurous or marvelous. Nothing is more gentle or strong. Nothing is more divine than love.

So, let us not shut ourselves within lonely chambers of illusive grander. May God grant us the faith to see greatness, the grace and courage to embrace it, and the humble love to daily realize our divine destiny. Let us be born into mangers and bear our crosses. This Christmas, may we live and die a thousand lives each and every day in the resurrected love of our Savior.

Let us be great. ●

Personal Reflections

● Whose definition of greatness are you pursuing:
the world's or Heaven's?
● What "crosses" and "mangers" has God placed in your life?
● Who are you serving with the love of Jesus today?

Hymn of Response

Sing We Now of Christmas

Sing we now of Christmas,
Noel, sing we here!
Hear our grateful praises
to the babe so dear.

Sing we Noel, the King is born, Noel!
Sing we now of Christmas, sing we now Noel!

Angels called to shepherds,
"Leave your flocks at rest,
journey forth to Bethlehem,
find the lambkin blest."

In Bethlehem they found him;
Joseph and Mary mild,
seated by the manger,
watching the holy child.

From the eastern country
came the kings afar,
bearing gifts to Bethlehem
guided by a star.

Gold and myrrh they took there,
gifts of greatest price;
there was ne'er a place on earth
so like paradise.

Sing we Noel, the King is born, Noel!
Sing we now of Christmas, sing we now Noel!

—15th Century French Folk Hymn, Author Unknown

December 16

Scriptural Interlude: The "I AMs"

Genesis 17:1

When Abram was ninety-nine years old, the Lord appeared to Abram and said to him, "**I am Almighty God**; walk before Me and be blameless."

Exodus 3:14

And God said to Moses, "**I AM WHO I AM.**" And He said, "Thus you shall say to the children of Israel, 'I AM has sent me to you.'"

John 8:58

Jesus said to them, "Most assuredly, I say to you, **before Abraham was, I AM.**"

John 6:35

And Jesus said to them, "**I am the bread of life.** He who comes to Me shall never hunger, and he who believes in Me shall never thirst."

John 8:12

Then Jesus spoke to them again, saying, "**I am the light of the world.** He who follows Me shall not walk in darkness, but have the light of life."

John 10:7–9

Then Jesus said to them again, "Most assuredly, I say to you, **I am the door of the sheep.** All who ever came before Me are thieves and robbers, but the sheep did not hear them. **I am the door.** If anyone enters by Me, he will be saved, and will go in and out and find pasture."

John 10:11 & 14

"**I am the good shepherd.** The good shepherd gives His life for the sheep."

"**I am the good shepherd**; and I know My sheep, and am known by My own."

John 11:25–26

Jesus said to her, "**I am the resurrection and the life.** He who believes in Me, though he may die, he shall live. And whoever lives and believes in Me shall never die. Do you believe this?"

John 14:6

Jesus said to him, "**I am the way, the truth, and the life.** No one comes to the Father except through Me."

John 15:1 & 5

"**I am the true vine**, and My Father is the vinedresser."

"**I am the vine**, you are the branches. He who abides in Me, and I in him, bears much fruit; for without Me you can do nothing."

Revelation 1:8

"**I am the Alpha and the Omega, the Beginning and the End**," says the Lord, "**who is and who was and who is to come, the Almighty**."

Revelation 1:17–18

And when I saw Him, I fell at His feet as dead. But He laid His right hand on me, saying to me, "Do not be afraid; **I am the First and the Last. I am He who lives, and was dead,** and behold, **I am alive forevermore**. Amen. And I have the keys of Hades and of Death.

Revelation 21:6

And He said to me, "It is done! **I am the Alpha and the Omega, the Beginning and the End.** I will give of the fountain of the water of life freely to him who thirsts."

December 17

Creation Defined

"The first fact that you must grasp is this: the renewal of creation has been wrought by the Self-same Word Who made it in the beginning. There is thus no inconsistency between creation and salvation for the One Father has employed the same Agent for both works, effecting the salvation of the world through the same Word Who made it in the beginning."

—Athanasius (296–373), *On the Incarnation*

"Advent creates people . . . new people."

—Dietrich Bonhoeffer (1906–1945),
sermon from December 3, 1933

In the beginning was the Word, and the Word was with God, and the Word was God.

—John 1:1

Creation Defined

W ords. Words speak. Words define. Words measure. Words name. Words describe. Words imagine. Words destroy. Words restore. The power of our words is unimaginable. Words form the fabric of our relationships. Words begin and end wars. Through words, our voices lay claim upon a piece of the world. Through words, our thoughts take form. Words are the ambassadors of ideas. Words are the currency of expression. Words are the projection of our inner-most feelings into the outer world. Words are the basis of our perception. Words are the language of understanding. Words are the most creative force in the universe. Without words, existence is absurd.

By the omnipotent Word, the cosmos began—spoken into existence out of nothing. Through the sheer expression of God's thought, molecules and galaxies were composed and the universe was called into being. When all was dark, the Light of the Creator's Word divided darkness. When all was formless and void, the tablets of the cosmic constitution prescribed the natural order and moral code. The Word's creative power separated sky from sea, defined the shores' boundaries, beckoned mountains to rise in worship and valleys to kneel in humble admiration. Creation danced to life when the Word's divine signature programed His Logos into every strand of DNA. The world was created and is even now sustained by the Word of God.

But unto a special race was the power of God's Word uniquely shared. For it alone would be ennobled with His image. Of all God's creatures that creep upon the earth, the gift of words was given to man exclusively. Elevated in both mind and stature, these semi-divine creatures were granted the Creator's power of words—creative expression, rational thought, and moral authority. Through the image of the Creator, humanity was empowered with grace to love, for it was His love that summoned man into existence and into fellowship with

Him. Man alone was charged with freedom and moral meaning. For it was unto man that the divine directive for creation was stewarded, and the power to break it was appointed solely unto his keep.

At a word, the world was destroyed. Through the lie, creative order was shattered, Heaven's language was forgotten, and fellowship was lost. The world fell into darkness. Life died. Separated from the Author, words lost their meaning and existence became absurd. The shadow of night descended upon the earth, and a dreadful silence muted our planet. Blessings turned to curses. All appeals to heaven fell upon the same ground that we would soon return. Holy creation groaned and human voices had not the power to unbind the spell. Human language could not undo the lie. Forgetting our native tongue, our words became merciless and without grace. Once loveless, they had lost their savor. Speech devolved into the boisterous noise of boasting gongs whose hollow rings echo of selfish nothingness. To dust we had returned . . .

As dust we would have remained had not the same Word who had first summoned us into being recalled us to life. The Creator spoke Himself into His creation. The Beginning and the End emerged into time. Definition entered the emptiness. The Architect became the Chief Cornerstone. The Author became the suffering hero in His own story. God became a baby, and the Word became flesh. The Word, which first spoke substance into the void, spoke light once again into the darkest recesses of our hearts and reimagined the world according to heaven's design.

Christmas re-creates all things to their true and proper places. Christmas is creation redefined. Christ has come to rearrange lives and to transform them into something heavenly; He is redefining all things. Through His Advent, God's Word reforms our lives. He who hears the Word of God and receives Him need never die. We, who by faith follow Christ and His call to love, become God's healing voice on earth. As Christmas comes again, let our words be few, and may the words we speak be those of our Savior—words of goodness, words of friendship, words of mercy, words of grace, words of truth—for man does not live by bread alone but by every Word that proceeds through the mouth of God. ●

And the Word became flesh and dwelt among us, and we beheld His glory, the glory as of the only begotten of the Father, full of grace and truth.

—John 1:14

Personal Reflections

- Whose words define your life?
- What opportunities will you have today to speak God's life-giving Word?

What Child Is This?

What Child is this who, laid to rest
On Mary's lap is sleeping?
Whom angels greet with anthems sweet,
While shepherds watch are keeping?
This, this is Christ the King,
Whom shepherds guard and angels sing;
Haste, haste, to bring Him laud,
The Babe, the Son of Mary.

Why lies He in such mean estate,
Where ox and ass are feeding?
Good Christians, fear, for sinners here
The silent Word is pleading.
Nails, spear shall pierce Him through,
The cross be borne for me, for you.
Hail, hail the Word made flesh,
The Babe, the Son of Mary.

So bring Him incense, gold and myrrh,
Come peasant, king to own Him;
The King of kings salvation brings,
Let loving hearts enthrone Him.
Raise, raise a song on high,

The virgin sings her lullaby.
Joy, joy for Christ is born,
The Babe, the Son of Mary.

—William Chatterton Dix (1865)

December 18

The Parchment of God

"You know what happens when a portrait that has been painted on a panel becomes obliterated through external stains. The artist does not throw away the panel, but the subject of the portrait has to come and sit for it again, and then the likeness is re-drawn on the same material. Even so it was with the All-holy Son of God. He, the Image of the Father, came down and dwelt in our midst, in order that He might renew mankind made after Himself, and seek out His lost sheep."

—Athanasius (296–373), *On the Incarnation*

"And in the Incarnation the whole human race recovers the dignity of the image of God . . . Through fellowship and communion with the incarnate Lord, we recover our true humanity, and at the same time we are delivered from that individualism which is the consequence of sin . . . By being partakers of Christ incarnate, we are partakers in the whole humanity which he bore . . . The incarnate Lord makes his followers the brothers of all mankind."

—Dietrich Bonhoeffer (1906–1945),
The Cost of Discipleship

The Parchment of God

We think in words, but in images we dream. Images shape understanding. Images give substance to the abstractions of thoughts. Images can be held. They color and texture perceptions. Images are the tangible examples of ideas. It is through our imagination that we see new possibilities of what can or should be drawn. We are undeniably drawn to images. But the images we behold draw us. They are the pictures and forms to which we pattern our souls. The essence of who we are is drawn by the capacity and light of our imaginations.

An image beheld beckons us towards new beauties, fresh truth, and abounding life; or, it leads us towards shameful regrets, rotting deception, and rancid death.

The identity of who we are is either astonishingly brushed to everlasting life by the creative hands of God or entombed within the narrow catacombs of human thought. Our present condition and our final end is either colored by God's grace through faith or faded by self-delusion inside the concentric circles and mirrored halls of narcissism.

What image will we behold? To what will we be conformed?

Long ago, when the world was new and good—freshly spoken from the Creator's imagination—God chose one creature and wove within its fabric the unique semblance of Himself. Of all the stars, in all the galaxies; of all the sunrises over all mountains, plains, and seas; of all that moves in the heavens above, or upon the face of earth, and all that is below it in the depths of its seas; God chose man to be the parchment upon which He would draw His self-portrait. Human beings were the marble into which he would carve His character. Man alone was engraved in the image and likeness of God.

Uniquely designed, personally touched by the loving hands of the

Creator, every human life has transcendent value that earthly scales cannot weigh.

For a time, our parents beheld the goodness of the Creator and reflected the brilliant radiance of His character, but when the tempter hissed the lie and the forbidden fruit was beheld and tasted, bitterness and woe dimmed creation. The loving authority of God was cast aside. The ugly idol of self was cast in His place.

Imagination went dark. Separated from God, the soul lost its awareness. Morality lost its direction. Freedom spiraled into ruin. Love deformed to envy. Reason fell into confusion. Creativity became decadent. Existence thinned, and Life paled of death. So it was that we who are the divine image-bearers became the self-image casters and consumers of sin and death.

Through evil of our own devising, we are no longer capable of rightly imagining the world. We cannot rightly conceive even ourselves. For how could we ever be ourselves once we have forgotten who we are? How much less are we able to perceive heaven?

Losing sight of God and beholding our icons of sin, we not only lose ourselves, we conform to the wrongs we imagine, even as we claim we are discovering who we are. Absent of God, we identify with sin. But sin is a false attempt to recast our essence and image according to a lie. Sin's bitter irony is that it is never an act of self-expression or authenticity. Sin is always a confused and cowardly act of becoming less than our true selves. Sin is never an act of becoming, but one of unbecoming. Even our most cherished and embedded sins are a deadly denial of who we really are, for we do not create ourselves. Sin's imagination can only lead to death.

Nevertheless, etchings of an ageless portrait remain traced upon the dry and dying parchment of human souls. Though the fabric has stretched and is torn, the dye has not faded. The image stubbornly remains, as though it were somehow even more real than the canvas upon which it was painted. The divine likeness and character was more substantial than the brittle marble into which it was shaped. The divine melody was louder than all the voices that ever sang its tune. The icon was more real than the fleshly vessel into which it was placed. God's likeness is more lasting than human sin.

God's image remains unaffected from sin's decay. But we—buried under millennia of selfishness, be-frailed by narcissism's toxic spell, weathered by sin—no longer possess the strength or grace to bear the majesty of God's sacred character without shame. Nor have we the sanctifying creativity to curate our intended selves. We lack the skill to recast our souls to life. Lost in sin's bleakness, we cannot imagine salvation.

And what we cannot imagine, we cannot realize.

But eye has not seen, nor ear heard, nor have entered into the imagination of man the things God has in store. When all hope was lost, the imagination of God that first spoke creation into being through His invisible Word, wove Himself into the fabric of humanity. God sculpted His Son into the frail dry and dusty clay of man.

"The Word became flesh and dwelt among us and we beheld His glory, the glory as of the only begotten of the Father full of grace and truth."

Christ is the image of the invisible God, the Firstborn over all creation. When we could no longer rightly imagine God or ourselves, God composed Himself into creation's symphony. At Bethlehem, God wove Himself into the tapestries of time. Unto all, who by faith, behold the baby in Bethlehem—Who was from eternity, born and crucified, and resurrected for our salvation—God refurbishes His unfading image. Because of Christ's Advent, we can be ourselves again.

God first beckoned the world to life through the speaking of words. But the second creation of the world began when the Word became an Image and all of creation will be reimagined to life.

"As heavens are higher than the earth so my ways are above your ways." The image of Christmas and the example of Jesus are ever before us, and the imago Dei brightly endures in even our darkest days. For all who have simply believed in Heaven's Son, the eternal future of Heaven's gift is certain.

To which image will we behold? Unto which image will we conform?

The image of Christ and the image of self are equally before us.

Every breath until our final respiration is pregnant with divine love ready to burst unto life, even as each moment is fraught with the temptation to exalt our self in shallow kingdoms of darkness.

Let us behold the splendor of our Savior. Let us behold the Image of the invisible God. Let us behold Him who was before all things; He is now born to you this Christmas day. Let us see Him and so conform ourselves to the One who came from Heaven and is lying in a manger. ●

Then God said, "Let Us make man in Our image, according to Our likeness; let them have dominion over the fish of the sea, over the birds of the air, and over the cattle, over all the earth and over every creeping thing that creeps on the earth." So God created man in His own image; in the image of God He created him; male and female He created them.

—Genesis 1:26-27

When I consider Your heavens, the work of Your fingers, The moon and the stars, which You have ordained, What is man that You are mindful of him, And the son of man that You visit him?

—Psalm 8:3-4

Personal Reflections

- Which image do you most often behold?
  - To whose image do you conform?
  - What sins mask your true identity?
- How does Advent give you your true self?
- How can you honor God with the self He gave you today?

Hymn of Response

O Come All Ye Faithful

O come, all ye faithful, joyful and triumphant,
O come ye, O come ye to Bethlehem!
Come, and behold Him, born the King of angels!

O come, let us adore Him;
O come, let us adore Him;
O come, let us adore Him, Christ, the Lord!

Sing, choirs of angels; sing in exultation;
sing, all ye citizens of heav'n above!
Glory to God, all glory in the highest!

Yea, Lord, we greet Thee, born this happy morning;
Jesus, to Thee be all glory giv'n!
Word of the Father, now in flesh appearing!

O come, let us adore Him;
O come, let us adore Him;
O come, let us adore Him, Christ, the Lord!

—17th Century Praise (Latin)
—translated John Francis Wade (18th Century)

December 19

An Advent Homily

St. John Chrysostom (349–407)
(Translator Unknown)

Behold a new and wondrous mystery. My ears resound to the Shepherd's song, piping no soft melody, but chanting full forth a heavenly hymn. The Angels sing. The Archangels blend their voice in harmony. The Cherubim hymn their joyful praise. The Seraphim exalt His glory. All join to praise his holy feast, beholding the Godhead here on earth, and man in heaven. He Who is above, now for our redemption dwells here below; and he that was lowly is by divine mercy raised.

Bethlehem this day resembles heaven; hearing from the stars the singing of angelic voices; and in place of the sun, enfolds within itself on every side, the Sun of justice. And ask not how: for where God wills, the order of nature yields. For He willed, He had the power, He descended, He redeemed; all things yielded in obedience to God. This day He Who is, is Born; and He Who is, becomes what He was not. For when He was God, He became man; yet not departing from the Godhead that is His. Nor yet by any loss of divinity became He man, nor through increase became He God from man; but being the Word

He became flesh, His nature, because of impassability, remaining unchanged.

And so the kings have come, and they have seen the heavenly King that has come upon the earth, not bringing with Him Angels, nor Archangels, nor Thrones, nor Dominations, nor Powers, nor Principalities, but, treading a new and solitary path, He has come forth from a spotless womb.

Since this heavenly birth cannot be described, neither does His coming amongst us in these days permit of too curious scrutiny. Though I know that a Virgin this day gave birth, and I believe that God was begotten before all time, yet the manner of this generation I have learned to venerate in silence and I accept that this is not to be probed too curiously with wordy speech. For with God we look not for the order of nature, but rest our faith in the power of Him who works.

What shall I say to you; what shall I tell you? I behold a Mother who has brought forth; I see a Child come to this light by birth. The manner of His conception I cannot comprehend.

Nature here rested, while the Will of God labored. O ineffable grace! The Only Begotten, Who is before all ages, Who cannot be touched or be perceived, Who is simple, without body, has now put on my body, that is visible and liable to corruption. For what reason? That coming amongst us he may teach us, and teaching, lead us by the hand to the things that men cannot see. For since men believe that the eyes are more trustworthy than the ears, they doubt of that which they do not see, and so He has deigned to show Himself in bodily presence, that He may remove all doubt.

Christ, finding the holy body and soul of the Virgin, builds for Himself a living temple, and as He had willed, formed there a man from the Virgin; and, putting Him on, this day came forth; unashamed of the lowliness of our nature'. For it was to Him no lowering to put on what He Himself had made. Let that handiwork be forever glorified, which became the cloak of its own Creator. For as in the first creation of flesh, man could not be made before the clay had come into His hand, so neither could this corruptible body be glorified, until it had first become the garment of its Maker.

What shall I say! And how shall I describe this Birth to you? For this wonder fills me with astonishment. The Ancient of days has become an infant. He Who sits upon the sublime and heavenly Throne, now lies in a manger. And He Who cannot be touched, Who is simple, without complexity, and incorporeal, now lies subject to the hands of men. He Who has broken the bonds of sinners, is now bound by an infant's bands. But He has decreed that ignominy shall become honor, infamy be clothed with glory, and total humiliation the measure of His Goodness.

For this He assumed my body, that I may become capable of His Word; taking my flesh, He gives me His spirit; and so He bestowing and I receiving, He prepares for me the treasure of Life. He takes my flesh, to sanctify me; He gives me His Spirit, that He may save me.

Come, then, let us observe the Feast. Truly wondrous is the whole chronicle of the Nativity. For this day the ancient slavery is ended, the devil confounded, the demons take to flight, the power of death is broken, paradise is unlocked, the curse is taken away, sin is removed from us, error driven out, truth has been brought back, the speech of kindliness diffused, and spreads on every side, a heavenly way of life has been 'in planted on the earth, angels communicate with men without fear, and men now hold speech with angels.

Why is this? Because God is now on earth, and man in heaven; on every side all things commingle. He became Flesh. He did not become God. He was God. Wherefore He became flesh, so that He Whom heaven did not contain, a manger would this day receive. He was placed in a manger, so that He, by whom all things are nourished, may receive an infant's food from His Virgin Mother. So, the Father of all ages, as an infant at the breast, nestles in the virginal arms, that the Magi may more easily see Him. Since this day the Magi too have come, and made a beginning of withstanding tyranny; and the heavens give glory, as the Lord is revealed by a star.

To Him, then, Who out of confusion has wrought a clear path, to Christ, to the Father, and to the Holy Ghost, we offer all praise, now and forever. Amen. ●

December 20

The Silence

"Lord, it is nearly midnight and I am waiting for You in the
 darkness and the great silence."

   —Thomas Merton (1915–1968), *"Thou Art Not as I Have
   Conceived Thee"*—a Christmas prayer at Midnight Mass

"The Father spoke one Word, which was His Son;
And this Word He always speaks in eternal silence;
And in silence It must be heard by the soul."

                    —St. John of the Cross (1542–1591),
                         "Sayings of Light and Love"

---

*"Awake! Why do You sleep, O Lord?
Arise! Do not cast us off forever.
Why do You hide Your face,
And forget our affliction and oppression?*

Redeem us for Your mercies' sake."

—Psalm 44:23-24, 26

The Silence

A quiet dread disturbs our spirits.
A soundless affliction numbs our souls.
A soft stillness stops our hearts.

Silence

That unbearable burden we cannot unload

Silence

That empty tension we cannot resolve

Silence

Our ever-present reminder that we are alone

The world is silent.
The universe is silent.
The heavens are silent.
And in their Silence,
    we linger.

Waiting for a word
waiting for a sign
waiting to find
waiting to be found
waiting to belong
waiting for anything
    to dispel our feelings of solitude.

But the Silence offers no comfort.
It does not break our fall.
Silence is indifferent to our desires.
It cares not for our concerns.
Silence is unmoved by our cries.
Silence is mute,
    deaf to our prayers.

In effort to be heard and avoid the Silence we inhabit the Noise.

Noise distracts us from our quiet despondency.
Noise becomes our coping.
Noise becomes our habit.

We fill our mouths with its gossip.
We stuff our ears with its chatter.
We pound our hearts with its vanity.
We fill our heads with its fitful thoughts.
We exhaust our days with its hurry, lest we catch our solitary reflection.

But noise is meaningless sound
    more empty
    more exhausting than Silence.

Even as the Noise fills our ears, it is only the dying reverberations of
empty echoes. Far from making us heard, the Habit of Noise deafens us
to the simplicity of Silence and the possibility of speech.

At the end of our hurry, Silence always waits.
The Silence soundlessly swallows all Noise.
For all the words we speak are just words.
All the treasures we chase are just toys.
All our thoughts are confused. All our passions contradict.
And all the fury we muster does not liberate our souls from solitude.

The Silence never stirs.

It persists
    just as empty
    ever mute
    forever cold

    fading all our echoes

    muting all our words
        to Silence

There is but one Word who can break the eternal Silence.
And He has spoken.

The Divine Word has come to earth and given His voice to Man.
Steeped in mystery and full of wonder.

As a man, God spoke to Man.
And it is in His Word alone that Man is not alone.
It is in His Word alone that Man is heard and found.
It is in His Word alone that Man has something to say.
For the Word alone is Life. And the word, that the Word forever speaks,
is everlasting love.

Every word but the Word is noise.
In Bethlehem, the Word has spoken.
It was there that the unbreakable Silence was broken.

In the Word, God and Man are one.

And yet a loneliness remains.
For though He came to His own, His own did not recognize Him. In our
dreadful aversion to silence, we did not hear the sound of His voice.

In our hurry, we pass Him by.
Amidst our Noise, we hear not His whispers.

Beneath the burden of our heavy solitude we do not lift our eyes to see
our Savior.

But God has spoken.
And God is speaking.

The same Word
that spoke the world in the beginning,
that spoke the light at Bethlehem,
speaks to us today.

Be still my soul and listen to God.
Silence yourself, for He is not far off.
And in His presence, you are never alone.

Can we not hear Him calling our name?
Can we not hear the love in His voice?
Can we not hear His call to love one another?
If we hear not His voice, we must slow our hurry and quiet our Noise.

The etiquette of Heaven very well may be that only one speaks at a time.
And if our souls are full of noise then God will patiently honor our
chatter and not interrupt our babblings.

But if we stop our mouths, tune our ears, and still our restless hearts,
even for a moment we can hear His voice, receive His love, and enjoy
the fellowship of His Word.

In silence we receive Jesus.
In our silence Jesus comes to us.

This Christmas let us not hurry.
Let us not be noisy.
Let us quiet and hush our thoughts.
Let our prayers be prayers of listening.

For Christ is come,
and in the stillness
and the silence,
our hearts can hear gentle voice of God.

Be still, and know that I am God;
I will be exalted among the nations,
I will be exalted in the earth!

—Psalm 46:10

But the Lord is in His holy temple.
Let all the earth keep silence before Him.

—Habakkuk 2:20

Personal Reflections

- **Are you more comfortable in Noise or in Silence?**
- **Regardless of your circumstances, how can you enjoy silence with God this Advent?**

Hymn of Response

Let All Mortal Flesh Keep Silence

Let all mortal flesh keep silence,
and with fear and trembling stand;
Ponder nothing earthly-minded,
for with blessing in his Hand
Christ our God to earth descendeth,
our full homage to demand.

King of kings, yet born of Mary,
as of old on earth he stood,
Lord of lords, in human vesture
– in the body and the blood
– He will give to all the faithful
his own self for heavenly food.

Rank on rank the host of heaven
spreads its vanguard on the way,
As the Light of Light descendeth
from the realms of endless day,
That the powers of hell may vanish
as the darkness clears away.

At his feet the six-winged seraph
– cherubim, with sleepless eye,
Veil their faces to the Presence,
as with ceaseless voice they cry,
"Alleluia, Alleluia, Alleluia, Lord Most High."

— 4th Century Hymn of the Early Church,
Author Unknown

December 21

Scriptural Interlude: The Christologies

John 1:1–14

In the beginning was the Word, and the Word was with God, and the Word was God. He was in the beginning with God. All things were made through Him, and without Him nothing was made that was made. In Him was life, and the life was the light of men. And the light shines in the darkness, and the darkness did not comprehend it.

There was a man sent from God, whose name was John. This man came for a witness, to bear witness of the Light, that all through him might believe. He was not that Light, but was sent to bear witness of that Light. That was the true Light which gives light to every man coming into the world.

He was in the world, and the world was made through Him, and the world did not know Him. He came to His own, and His own did not receive Him. But as many as received Him, to them He gave the right to become children of God, to those who believe in His name: who were born, not of blood, nor of the will of the flesh, nor of the will of man, but of God.

And the Word became flesh and dwelt among us, and we beheld His glory, the glory as of the only begotten of the Father, full of grace and truth.

John bore witness of Him and cried out, saying, "This was He of whom I said, 'He who comes after me is preferred before me, for He was before me.'" And of His fullness we have all received, and grace for grace. For the law was given through Moses, but grace and truth came through Jesus Christ. No one has seen God at any time. The only begotten Son, who is in the bosom of the Father, He has declared Him.

Philippians 2:5–10

Let this mind be in you which was also in Christ Jesus, who, being in the form of God, did not consider it robbery to be equal with God, but made Himself of no reputation, taking the form of a bondservant, and coming in the likeness of men. And being found in appearance as a man, He humbled Himself and became obedient to the point of death, even the death of the cross.

Therefore God also has highly exalted Him and given Him the name which is above every name, that at the name of Jesus every knee should bow, of those in heaven, and of those on earth, and of those under the earth, and that every tongue should confess that Jesus Christ is Lord, to the glory of God the Father.

Colossians 1:13–18

He has delivered us from the power of darkness and conveyed us into the kingdom of the Son of His love, in whom we have redemption through His blood, the forgiveness of sins.

He is the image of the invisible God, the firstborn over all creation. For by Him all things were created that are in heaven and that are on earth, visible and invisible, whether thrones or dominions or principalities or powers. All things were created through Him and for Him. And He is before all things, and in Him all things consist. And He is the head of the body, the church, who is the beginning, the firstborn from the dead, that in all things He may have the preeminence.

Hebrews 1:1–4

God, who at various times and in various ways spoke in time past to the fathers by the prophets, has in these last days spoken to us by His Son, whom He has appointed heir of all things, through whom also He made the worlds; who being the brightness of His glory and the express image of His person, and upholding all things by the word of His power, when He had by Himself purged our sins, sat down at the right hand of the Majesty on high, having become so much better than the angels, as He has by inheritance obtained a more excellent name than they.

Hebrews 2:17–18

Therefore, in all things He had to be made like His brethren, that He might be a merciful and faithful High Priest in things pertaining to God, to make propitiation for the sins of the people. For in that He Himself has suffered, being tempted, He is able to aid those who are tempted.

Jude 24–25

Now to Him who is able to keep you from stumbling,
And to present you faultless
Before the presence of His glory with exceeding joy,
To God our Savior,
Who alone is wise,
Be glory and majesty,
Dominion and power,
Both now and forever.
Amen.

December 22

Home

"Into this world, this demented inn in which there is absolutely no room for him at all, Christ comes uninvited. But because he cannot be at home in it, because he is out of place in it, his place is with those others for whom there is no room. His place is with those who do not belong, who are rejected by power because they are regarded as weak . . . With those for whom there is no room, Christ is present in this world."

—Thomas Merton (1915–1968),
"The Time of the End Is the Time of No Room."

If any of you are driven out to the farthest parts under heaven, from there the LORD your God will gather you, and from there He will bring you.

—Deuteronomy 30:4

Home

*H*ome was a place where all things lived in peace and harmony, where joy was full, everyone family—a place where love and laughter abounded, faces and hearts smiled in unity—a place of warmth, a place of rest, a place of belonging. But for those lost in ourselves, home cannot be found.

From the moment we entered this alien world, orphaned into a false existence, we have yet to experience its glow. Adrift—Bewildered—Forlorn—Ostracized—Outcast. We are banished creatures, exiled from a place we yearn for but have never seen. We hunger for an untasted dish and thirst for a wine that has never touched our lips. This stubborn desire plagues our thoughts and haunts our dreams. We spend our days in a surreal paradox, longing for a kingdom both familiar and strange.

Though its boundaries are far off and vague, home remains the center. For it is we who have overreached its borders. Though its customs and language strike our ears as dumb, it is we who are odd. Though it is uncharted by human minds and undiscovered by our straining gaze, it is we who are abstract and blind. Though its familiarity is eerie, it is we who are obscure and unknown. Its presence goes unrecognized because it is we who are absent. And still, fallen and flung out so very far beyond its orbit, we are beckoned and defined by its call, for the reality of home is more certain than the craven ache wrenching every heart for justice and love.

How did we get here? What oceans of sin did we cross? What vast expanses have our souls transgressed to come to the furthest reaches of nowhere? As refugees in time, driven by winds of ego and pride, we are scattered without bearing or direction. Which way do we go? How can we return? Where do we belong? Disoriented and afraid, we wander and wander and wander . . . Instead of welcome, we encounter a harsh strangeness and rancorous dis-ease. Endlessly drawing maps, our exhausted wisdom frays. Our fickle wills forge compasses attracted only to the most immediate objects. And so our instruments falter, our schemes endlessly circle round, and our vehicles take us further into wilderness. We search for home in vain.

Numb and afraid, we forget home, the One who made it, and we no longer recognize our divinely given name. The unfamiliar world and its pain become familiar. As we inhabit an unwelcoming world, we embrace the emptiness of our exile and erect dwellings unworthy of our true race, for in the desert of self, the only foundations are of sand. Devolving further, we acclimate to the toxic air that mortally poisons our souls. The acidity of sin mars the graceful image bestowed by the Divine Creator, and we who were once beautiful become hideous and unrecognizable.

Banished to a hostile land and distorted beyond recognition, disregarded and forgotten, self-abused and debased beyond worth, we become what was never intended and inhabit a world never meant to be.

But in our un-returnable exile, Home has come to us. Unfamiliar God became familiar to unfamiliar man. Though we were without identity, He went unrecognized when He came to His own. Bound by time, we did not fathom Eternity. Stooped with pride, we did not perceive the divine. In selfish apathy, we failed to conceive that God is love. Condemned to darkness and death, we could not comprehend the Light of Life. Lost in exile, we did not remember to Whom we belong. But Eternity entered time. The Maker of all things dwelt among us. Divine love traversed galaxies of sin. Immortal God assumed mortal flesh, and Life was born to die so that through His death, we, the dead, might live. Heaven came to earth to banish our exile and to bring us home.

Jesus is the Way, the Truth, and the Life. Everywhere but Christ is exile. In Him alone, the refugee finds welcome. In Christ alone is home. By His sacrifice, our pardon is fully granted. In His Name, our citizenship is awarded. At His call, we are reborn to Life. Into His family, our adoption is sealed by His mighty love. By His scarred and skilled hands, our faces are redrawn to His heavenly likeness. Our

Father calls us by names that we have never heard but now unmistakably recognize as our own.

We are recalled home by God's gift of Christmas. He has given us home by giving us Himself. Belonging is the greatest gift Christmas offers. Because of Christmas, we need not wait for Heaven, for God makes His home in human hearts. Home was not found, for Home has found us and is now knocking at our doors. We need only to answer and dine. We need not languish in exile, for the banishment is broken, and we belong to God. We need not wait for Christmas for Christmas is arrived.

In the love of Christ, we are home—every moment of every day. This Christmas, let your forsaken soul be found, let your heart rest in God's house tonight, for you are the Father's daughter and the younger brother of Jesus. You are a precious child belonging to the eternal Family. Welcome home. ●

Personal Reflections

- Where do you seek belonging?
- How does Advent provide home?

Hymn of Response

God Rest Ye Merry Gentlemen

God rest ye merry, gentlemen
Let nothing you dismay
Remember, Christ, our Saviour
Was born on Christmas day
To save us all from Satan's power
When we were gone astray.

O tidings of comfort and joy,
Comfort and joy
O tidings of comfort and joy.

In Bethlehem, in Israel,
This blessèd Babe was born
And laid within a manger
Upon this blessed morn
The which His Mother Mary
Did nothing take in scorn.

From God our Heavenly Father
A blessed Angel came;
And unto certain Shepherds
Brought tidings of the same:

How that in Bethlehem was born
The Son of God by Name.

The shepherds at those tidings
Rejoiced much in mind,
And left their flocks a-feeding
In tempest, storm and wind:
And went to Bethlehem straightway
This blessed Babe to find.

But when to Bethlehem they came
Where at this infant lay,
They found Him in a manger,
Where oxen feed on hay;
His Mother Mary kneeling,
Unto the Lord did pray.

Now to the Lord sing praises,
All you within this place,
And with true love and brotherhood
Each other now embrace;
This holy tide of Christmas
All other doth deface.

O tidings of comfort and joy,
Comfort and joy
O tidings of comfort and joy.

—English Folk Hymn (16th Century)

104

A Heavenly Interlude: Book III of Paradise Lost

The following lines are excerpts from Book III of John Milton's *Paradise Lost*. It is a narration of a scene in Heaven, primarily consisting of a dialogue between the Father and the Son discussing the fate of man and God's marvelous and mysterious plan for his redemption.

> "Die hee or Justice must; unless for him
> Som other able, and as willing, pay
> The rigid satisfaction, death for death.
> Say, Heav'nly Powers, where shall we find such love,
> Which of ye will be mortal to redeem
> Mans mortal crime, and just th' unjust to save,
> Dwels in all Heaven charitie so deare?"
>
> He ask'd, but all the Heav'nly Quire stood mute,
> And silence was in Heav'n: on man's behalf
> Patron or Intercessor none appeerd,
> Much less that durst upon his own head draw
> The deadly forfeiture, and ransom set.
> And now without redemption all mankind

Must have bin lost, adjudg'd to Death and Hell
By doom severe, had not the Son of God,
In whom the fulness dwels of love divine,
His dearest mediation thus renewd.

"Father, thy word is past, man shall find grace."

". . . Behold mee then, mee for him, life for life
I offer, on mee let thine anger fall;
Account mee Man; I for his sake will leave
Thy bosom, and this glorie next to thee
Freely put off, and for him lastly die
Well pleas'd, on me let Death wreck all his rage . . .

". . . But I shall rise Victorious, and subdue
My Vanquisher, spoild of his vanted spoile;
Death his deaths wound shall then receive, & stoop
Inglorious, of his mortall sting disarm'd.
I through the ample Air in Triumph high
Shall lead Hell Captive maugre Hell, and show
The powers of darkness bound . . .

". . . So Heav'nly love shal outdoo Hellish hate."

December 24

The Paradox of Advent

"He by whom all things were made was made one of all things. The Son of God by the Father without a mother became the Son of man by a mother without a father. The Word Who is God before all time became flesh at the appointed time. The maker of the sun was made under the sun. He Who fills the world lays in a manger, great in the form of God but tiny in the form of a servant; this was in such a way that neither was His greatness diminished by His tininess, nor was His tininess overcome by His greatness."

—St. Augustine (354–430), *Sermon 187*

"The Son of God became man so that men might become sons of God."

—Athanasius (296–373), *On the Incarnation*

For whoever desires to save his life will lose it, but whoever loses his life for My sake will save it."

—Luke 9:24

The Paradox of Advent

Advent is the paradox that bridges Heaven and Earth. It is the hinge upon which recorded time and eternity both swing. God's coming is the before and after of our faith. Advent marks the birth of our Lord Jesus Christ—the One who would die for the sins of the world, the One whom God would raise from the grave, the One who would ascend to the right hand of His Father in Heaven. Advent is God's argument that the world, broken and wayward as it has become, can be redeemed. Advent beacons Hope. Advent summons Peace. Advent elicits Joy. But the biggest wonder of Advent is God's amazing Love.

Consider the many paradoxes of God's love resonating within the most paradoxical statement ever sounded on human tongues.

"οὕτως γὰρ ἠγάπησεν ὁ θεὸς τὸν κόσμον..."

"For God so loved the world ..."

God's love for humanity is paradoxical. The One who is Great and Worthy gives affection and attentive care for the undeserving, while the unworthy rudely shun Majesty. The world, by right, ought to love God, but we, in fact, have made ourselves His enemy. God, by earthly right, ought to condemn His rebellious creation, but He loves us despite our enmity.

"ὥστε τὸν υἱὸν τὸν μονογενῆ ἔδωκεν..."

"...that His only-begotten Son He gave..."

Towers and Babels abound as the world strives to exalt ourselves to be like God, but God lowers Himself to be like us. Man was made in God's image, but out of love, God makes Himself into human likeness and form.

The long history of human religions consists of little more than man offering futile sacrifices to appease angry gods. But no sacrifice is found to bridge sin's ever widening chasm. Our offenses are too great, our offerings too meager, and our altars too profane. And yet in these words, we do not see guilty man making satisfaction on his behalf for his offense against God. Rather, we see God, who was both innocent and the offended, paradoxically sacrificing Himself—to Himself—to make satisfaction for man.

Even more astonishingly, what father is there among men who would not ransom all that he possessed for the life of his son? Is it not incomprehensible then how the Father does not give a ransom for His Son but gives His Son as our Ransom?

"ἵνα πᾶς ὁ πιστεύων εἰς αὐτὸν μὴ ἀπόληται ἀλλ' ἔχῃ ζωὴω αἰώνιον."

"...so that anyone who believes in Him shall not perish, but have life everlasting."

The immortal Son perished so that mortals could have everlasting life. The costly grace of God is freely given. That which could never be earned is available for the asking. The most valuable commodity—purchased at the dearest price—is graciously supplied on faith alone. Life and forgiveness, which are most sought, are most readily abundant. And the wonder of it all is that God did not come to condemn the wayward world but to save it.

Advent is the fullest expression, the most personal embodiment, and the complete reaffirmation of God's Love for the good creation He summoned from nothing long ago.

What a paradox is our God! What manner of paradox bought our salvation!

Advent is birthed in paradox

The scandalous miracle of the Virgin Birth—the Incarnation of the Word becoming Flesh—the fullness of God becoming fully Man—the humble emptying of Majesty that the lowly may be exalted and filled—the Son's forsaking of Heaven for the forsaken on Earth—the Immortal donning mortality—the Wisdom that both made and holds the cosmos now weak, inarticulate Babe.

Advent dies in paradox

The convicted convicting the Pardoner—Creation condemning its Creator—God as Criminal—the slaying of Immortal Life—Man's Murder of God—God forsaking Himself—the Innocent, Incarnate Word of God becoming the embodiment and incarnation of all the world's sin and guilt—the Holy One now the person of Blasphemy—the Heavenly Man ravaged by Hell—the Blessed One becoming the Curse—the well-pleasing Son becoming the sole object of His Father's relentless wrath—Omnipotence surrendering to defeat.

Advent rises in paradox

The death of dying—mortality swallowed by Immortality—hate melted by mercy—sorrow succumbs to joy—apathy transforms to love—the most unrighteous act in all eternity grants righteousness unto all who believe—the greatest act of evil is redeemed to become our greatest good—that which was dead reborn to life—that which was lost now is found—those who were doomed reclaimed by divine destiny.

Advent ascends in paradox

The Son of Man returns to Heaven—the new Kingdom begins with the physical absence of the King—eternity dawns with the Light of the World shining inward—the exterior empire of Rome remains inescapably apparent, while the immaterial Kingdom of Heaven is invisible without faith. The kings of this earth fret and are no more, while Heaven's lowest servants are commissioned by the One who has been granted all authority. We corruptible temples, now in-dwelt by the Incorruptible Fire.

We are children of Christmas, paradoxically reborn at Bethlehem. But God's love for the world resounding from Heaven to Bethlehem to Calvary to Kingdom Come does not end with Advent. We live and move and have our being amidst this wonderful paradox of God's love. Serving others is the exalted path to greatness. Turning the other cheek is the most decisive action. Sacrificing our preferences and laying down our lives for our neighbor's good is our surest guarantee of gain.

Only the poor in spirit are rich enough to possess the kingdom of heaven. Only the pure in heart have the strength to look upon the face of God. Only those who starve for righteousness find food to fill them. Only the humble are bold enough to inherit the earth. Only those who dare to long for things beyond what this world has to offer receive Heaven's blessings and joys. God's love has turned the wisdom of this world upside down. For we walk by faith and not by sight. We, like our Savior, lose our lives to find our souls in Him. Hell's redeemed are the world's co-redeemers and Heaven's heirs.

For we, Christ's redeemed, are the beacons of this amazing Hope. We are the heralds of the lasting Peace, which is forever reconciling Heaven and Earth. We are citizens of the Joyful kingdom who, through the momentary trials of this life, stagger onward rejoicing towards our eternal prize. We are the bearers of Heaven's gracious Love reawakening a drowsy world to glory.

May we celebrate this Advent by loving one another with Heaven's paradoxical love that God has so richly poured into our hearts. ●

For God so loved the world, that He gave His only begotten Son, that whosoever believes in Him shall not perish, but have everlasting life.

Personal Reflections

- What paradoxes of God most marvel you, drawing your heart to worship?
- How does your life reflect the paradoxes of Advent?

* The translations of John 3:16 beneath the Greek text are the author's.

Hymn of Response

Of the Father's Love Begotten

Of the Father's love begotten,
Ere the worlds began to be,
He is Alpha and Omega,
He the source, the ending He,
Of the things that are, that have been,
And that future years shall see,
Evermore and evermore!

At His Word the worlds were framed;
He commanded; it was done:
Heaven and earth and depths of ocean
In their threefold order one;
All that grows beneath the shining
Of the moon and burning sun,
Evermore and evermore!

He is found in human fashion,
Death and sorrow here to know,
That the race of Adam's children
Doomed by law to endless woe,
May not henceforth die and perish

In the dreadful gulf below,
Evermore and evermore!

O that birth forever blessed,
When the virgin, full of grace,
By the Holy Ghost conceiving,
Bore the Saviour of our race;
And the Babe, the world's Redeemer,
First revealed His sacred face,
evermore and evermore!

O ye heights of heaven adore Him;
Angel hosts, His praises sing;
Powers, dominions, bow before Him,
and extol our God and King!
Let no tongue on earth be silent,
Every voice in concert sing,
Evermore and evermore!

This is He Whom seers in old time
Chanted of with one accord;
Whom the voices of the prophets
Promised in their faithful word;
Now He shines, the long expected,
Let creation praise its Lord,
Evermore and evermore!

Christ, to Thee with God the Father,
And, O Holy Ghost, to Thee,

Hymn and chant with high thanksgiving,
And unwearied praises be:
Honour, glory, and dominion,
And eternal victory,
Evermore and evermore!

—Aurelius Prudentius (348–413)
—Translated by J. M. Neale (1818–1866)
& Henry W. Baker (1821–1877)

December 25

Cosmic Dawn

"God is on earth! He is among men! Not in the fire, nor amid the sound of trumpets; not in the smoking mountain, nor in the darkness; nor in the terrible and roaring tempest giving the Law, but manifested in the flesh. The gentle and good One dwells with those He condescends to make His equals! God is in the flesh, not operating from a distance, as did the prophets, but through Him human nature, one with ours. He seeks to bring back all mankind to Himself."

—St. Basil (329–379), *On the Incarnation*

"Jesus was God and man in one person, that God and man might be happy together again."

—George Whitfield (1714–1770), from his sermons

And, having come in, the angel said to her,
"Rejoice, highly favored one, the Lord is with you;
blessed are you among women!"

—Luke 2:28

Cosmic Dawn

The most cosmic moment in history occurred in the most ordinary of ways.

Life is incredibly boring. We have ups and downs, moments of pride and regret, but nothing too spectacular ever happens. We do not particularly stand out. Only those closest to us ever learn to appreciate our unique subtleties. To the wider world, we are an invisible enigma, never to even be puzzled over or solved. We hardly make the news, much less history. And so goes our lives, unnoticed by the world, far removed from the great and famous figures that give it substance and shape.

We are too weighed down by drudgery to be worthy of greatness. Our best energy is drained in the thankless tasks of changing diapers, repairing leaky faucets, figuring our taxes, and mowing our lawns. Our time is spent waiting—waiting for something—waiting for nothing in particular, anticipating a vague tomorrow. In a cyclical monotony, we wake, we work, we eat, we sleep. Day after day, month after month, year after year, decade after decade until we are no more. Life has been thus for centuries. For everyone not named Caesar or Kardashian, life is entirely pedestrian.

Such was the case for an ordinary girl, with an ordinary name, in an utterly unremarkable town. In a moment, her ordinary routine was interrupted with startling news from another world. She would miraculously be with an entirely unordinary child who would save His people. Rumors naturally spread. The people of her village, as in any other, were too engrossed with the ordinary to believe anything to the contrary. To them, as it would have been with us, what was remarkable was the scandal, not the sacred life within her.

To them, as with us, what made headlines was capitol news—the royal decree to register. For some, for this girl and her betrothed, this meant traveling afar. After a weary journey, their destination was clogged with people—with no place prepared to receive them or their quickly-coming child but a lowly stable—as Bethlehem travelers and innkeepers forgot their compassion—while the lost world was preoccupied with counting and being counted—a mother cried, and her baby was born. Those near and far took no note of the moment and continued on their way, failing to recognize the magnificence of such an "ordinary" event.

In nearby fields, it is told, shepherds were keeping watch, as always, over their flocks by night. It was to them alone that angelic choirs sang the announcement. A star shone bright declaring His glory, but almost no one looked to heaven or pondered its significance. From the emperor, to the priests, to subjects on the streets, no one but the tenders of sheep and foreigners from the East came to see the God-babe. Christmas forever changed the world, but the world was too busy being ordinary to appreciate the most cosmic event in history.

Christmas is not an isolated incident. Advent preludes eternity. Christmas is the opening act of a total reconfiguration of the cosmos. Heaven and earth are inextricably united. God's arrival has made all things new. Every second is sacred. Have we the hope to live with radiance in such a radically new reality? Must we hold back in ordinary doubt? Must we define our lives by our ordinary apathies and fears? Must heaven wait when Christmas has come and God is now with us? In the monotonous mundacities of life lies the secret of eternity. Can we not see that the most ordinary moments in our lives are loaded with cosmic dynamite? Christmas is the moment time exploded with eternity, and the present is our chance to join the cosmic symphony.

Christmas tells us that we find our greatness only when we become like God, by serving others instead of ourselves. The flicker of fame is already whisking away, and the sun is setting on history as God draws all things unto Himself. But because of Christmas, obscurity is fleeting, and glory is forever for those who silence stones by proclaiming Christ through heaven's song of sacrificial serving and love. Life now begins, punctured by cosmic interruptions. Heaven intrudes upon our every breath.

Are we so fond of our ordinary plans to notice? Are we so entrapped by the fictions inside our head that we miss the reality of Christ? Are we so busy building sandcastles that we are blind to God's eternal kingdom? Are we so bound by rules that we cannot fathom grace? Are we so proud to cowardly hide our hurts in darkness instead of humbly stepping into His healing light? Are we so selfish and small that we fail to imagine the magnificence of mercy? Life is before us. Life is now. Dare we to live? Have we the courage to love as God loves us?

Because of Christmas, eternity intersects every ordinary moment of the present. Because of Christmas, we, the ordinary, are now divine. ●

Personal Reflections

● **What ordinary moments are sacred to you and God?**

● **What sacred moments do you neglect for their commonness?**

● **What ordinary moments will you redeem today?**

Hymn of Response

The First Noel

The first Noel the angels did say
Was to certain poor shepherds in fields as they lay:
In fields where they lay keeping their sheep
On a cold winter's night that was so deep
Noel, Noel, Noel, Noel
Born is the King of Israel!

They looked up and saw a star
Shining in the east beyond them far
And to the earth it gave great light
And so it continued both day and night
Noel, Noel, Noel, Noel
Born is the King of Israel!

And by the light of that same star
Three Wise men came from country far
To seek for a King was their intent
And to follow the star wherever it went
Noel, Noel, Noel, Noel
Born is the King of Israel!

This star drew nigh to the northwest
O'er Bethlehem it took its rest
And there it did both stop and stay
Right o'er the place where Jesus lay
Noel, Noel, Noel, Noel
Born is the King of Israel!

—Author Unknown, 16th Century Cornish Folk Hymn

December 26

Scriptural Postscript: Living Beneath Bethlehem Skies

Psalm 37

Do not fret because of evildoers,
Nor be envious of the workers of iniquity.
For they shall soon be cut down like the grass,
And wither as the green herb.
Trust in the Lord, and do good;
Dwell in the land, and feed on His faithfulness.
Delight yourself also in the Lord,
And He shall give you the desires of your heart.
Commit your way to the Lord,
Trust also in Him,
And He shall bring it to pass.
He shall bring forth your righteousness as the light,
And your justice as the noonday.
Rest in the Lord, and wait patiently for Him;
Do not fret because of him who prospers in his way,
Because of the man who brings wicked schemes to pass.
Cease from anger, and forsake wrath;
Do not fret—it only causes harm . . .

Depart from evil, and do good;
And dwell forevermore.
For the Lord loves justice,
And does not forsake His saints;
They are preserved forever,
But the descendants of the wicked shall be cut off.
The righteous shall inherit the land,
And dwell in it forever . . .

Wait on the Lord,
And keep His way,
And He shall exalt you to inherit the land;
When the wicked are cut off, you shall see it . . .

But the salvation of the righteous is from the Lord;
He is their strength in the time of trouble.
And the Lord shall help them and deliver them;
He shall deliver them from the wicked,
And save them,
Because they trust in Him.

Micah 6:8

He has shown you, O man, what is good;
And what does the Lord require of you
But to do justly,
To love mercy,
And to walk humbly with your God?

Matthew 6:33

"But seek first the kingdom of God and His righteousness, and all these things shall be added to you."

Mark 12:29–31

Jesus answered him, "The first of all the commandments is: 'Hear, O Israel, the Lord our God, the Lord is one. And you shall love the Lord your God with all your heart, with all your soul, with all your mind, and with all your strength.' This is the first commandment. And the second, like it, is this: 'You shall love your neighbor as yourself.' There is no other commandment greater than these."

John 20:30–31

And truly Jesus did many other signs in the presence of His disciples, which are not written in this book; but these are written that you may believe that Jesus is the Christ, the Son of God, and that believing you may have life in His name.

Colossians 3:1–4

If then you were raised with Christ, seek those things which are above, where Christ is, sitting at the right hand of God. Set your mind on things above, not on things on the earth. For you died, and your life is hidden with Christ in God. When Christ who is our life appears, then you also will appear with Him in glory.

Matthew 28:18–20

And Jesus came and spoke to them, saying, "All authority has been given to Me in heaven and on earth. Go therefore and make disciples of all the nations, baptizing them in the name of the Father and of the Son and of the Holy Spirit, teaching them to observe all things that I have commanded you; and lo, I am with you always, even to the end of the age." Amen.

Acknowledgments

T hank you, Reader for picking up this book. Thank you for allowing me the privilege of being a part of your Christmas season. I hope these meditations have enriched your life and made Jesus's coming at Advent more meaningful to you. If it has, please know that this project would not have been possible without the constant encouragement and generous support from many different people. Thank you.

Thank you, students and staff of Midland Classical Academy. Thank you, congregation and staff at Midland Bible Church. Thank you for the opportunity to share what I've written each Christmas for the past twelve Decembers. Thank you for patient listening and kind words. Thank you.

Thank you, Vince Loftis. Thank you for giving me the idea of making this a book. This project would have never materialized had it not been for your initial nudge and your stubborn belief in me. Thank you for your friendship. Thank you.

Thank you, Matt Waller and General Echols. Thank you for listening to me between Santa Fe and Roswell as we returned from an epic weekend of fishing. You helped me form a dream into an actionable plan. Thank you.

Thank you Amber Struble. Thank you for spending a month of June creating an animated video out of the *Babel or Bethlehem* track. You did an amazing job bringing it to life. Thank you.

Thank you, Luke McDonald. Thank you for the years of playing music underneath live readings at MCA and Midland Bible. Thank you for creating the music you put to these tracks. Every tense chord and texture enhance its message and captures the emotional context in which it is shared. Thank you.

Thank you, Rachel Long. Thank you for using your gift of painting to visually express what my words are trying to say. I find something new each time I look over what you created. Thank you.

Thank you, BBS 2019 Focus Group. Thank you for reading the rough manuscript, gently pointing out mistakes, and winsomely offering suggestions. Your efforts enhanced the final product. Thank you.

Thank you Nancy Haight and Maddy D. Thank you for editing, proofing, and getting this book ready for print. Thank you.

Thank you, Ryan Scheife of Mayfly Design. Thank you for patiently teaching and explaining the process with me. Your consummate professionalism was equally matched by your artistry in the designing of the cover and layout of this book. Thank you for putting yourself into this project as though it were your own. Thank you.

Thank you, Kevin and Jill Sparks, Eric and Valerie Boyt, and Mark and Melissa Rae. Your encouragement and enthusiasm were a timely wind whenever my sails began to falter. Thank you.

Thank you, Jordan Weatherl. Thank you for "getting on the rollercoaster" and not jumping off—even when I wanted to. Thank you for your counsel. Thank you for your advice. I always looked forward to our reports, and always left clear headed and eager to act. Thank you.

Thank you, Rowan, Eli, and Selah. Even though you were not here when I first began to write these devotions, you each and in your own way wonderfully fill my life with perspective and joy. Your lives have touched me profoundly and made me a better writer. Thank you.

Thank you, Laura. Thank you for believing in me and this project. Thank you for your patience. Thank you for your love. Thank you for understanding me like no one else. I love you.

Thank you, Jesus Christ. Thank you for Christmas. Thank you for coming to earth, as a man, to redeem the world. Thank you for giving me these words to write. May your Kingdom be enlarged and may your Person be glorified by this offering. Thank you.

With gratitude,
Brandon Anthony Shuman

What Did You Think of Beneath Bethlehem Skies?

Thank you for purchasing and reading Beneath Bethlehem Skies.

I hope that it blessed you and made your Christmas more meaningful for you. If so, it would be really nice if you could share this book with your friends and family by posting to Facebook, Instagram, and Twitter

If you enjoyed these devotions and found some benefit in reading them, I'd like to hear from you and hope that you could take some time to post a review on Amazon. Your feedback and support will help me to greatly improve my writing craft for future projects and make this book even better.

I want you, the reader, to know that your review is very important and so, if you'd like to leave a review, please search and find Beneath Bethlehem Skies on Amazon.com and leave a review. Thank you very much!

I wish you Merry Christmas
and God's blessings in all your adventures!

The meditations of *Beneath Bethlehem Skies* can be experienced through a variety of platforms.

Books

Available in paperback, hard cover, and eBook, *Beneath Bethlehem Skies* is a contemplative Advent devotional comprised of twenty-six mediations reflecting upon the meaning and miracle of Jesus's birth. Stunning watercolors, by Rachel Long, beautifully adorn the original compositions of the hard cover and eBook versions.

Music

Listen to the devotions of *Beneath Bethlehem Skies* by streaming the digital album. Read by the author and his wife, ten meditations are set to thematic soundscapes composed by Luke McDonald, allowing the listener to discover additional meaning and hear new points of emphasis through musical insights and vocal inflections. *Beneath Bethlehem Skies* can be heard on Spotify, Pandora, Apple Music or wherever music is streamed. The album is also available in the iTunes store.

Live

Readings of *Beneath Bethlehem Skies* can be shared each Advent during worship services and family gatherings as believers reunite to celebrate the birth of Jesus. Whether they are read in the presence of large congregations or in more intimate settings, these corporate expressions enhance fellowship and community as they elevate thoughts and fill hearts with the wonder of Christmas.

To bring Beneath Bethlehem Skies *to your church this Christmas or to sign up for our newsletter please visit*

www.brandonanthonyshuman.com.

Follow us on the Bethlehem Skies Facebook page.

Made in the USA
Coppell, TX
04 December 2022

87806636R00079